Contents

Guide to the Documents

The Public Record Office classifies its many millions of documents by dividing them into groups for each ministry or government department from which they come, and then subdividing them into classes which reflect the different administrative functions that created the records or where necessary, the different types of document generated by the department's varied activities. The departmental groups are given letter codes (CAB for the Cabinet Office papers, HO for those of the Home Office and so on) and their classes are designated by numbers. The classes themselves contain hundreds, often thousands, of separate pieces, so that if you want to see a document at the Public Record Office you first have to discover its group letters, class and piece number. The Ministry of Information papers for the Second World War which form the basis of this publication are a rich and disparate collection. They are classified as follows:

INF 1 Files of Correspondence 1936-1946
990 brown manilla files containing manuscript, typescript, duplicated and sometimes printed reports, memoranda and correspondence. They include the following subsections:

1 – 159, 436 – 495, Administration
160 – 177, 496 – 520, Broadcasting
178 – 192, 521 – 540, Censorship
193 – 225   Film
226 – 248   General Publicity

249 – 260   Home Planning
261 – 293   Home Intelligence, including the files of the Wartime Social Survey. INF 1/292 consists of the weekly reports of the Home Intelligence Division of the Ministry, which gathered information about public opinion from all parts of the country and issued its weekly reports cyclo-styled on foolscap paper, usually running to about ten pages.
294 – 339   Home Publicity
340 – 345   Campaigns
346 – 350   Literary and Editorial
351 – 357   Photographs
708 – 758   Pre-war Publicity
844 – 944   Ministerial

INF 2 Guard Books : publicity
74 large volumes containing general printed publicity material, leaflets, photographs, posters etc. One volume (INF 2/19) contains examples of US propaganda in various languages, and a large proportion of the class consists of British propaganda in foreign languages, aimed at almost every part of the world. The last nineteen volumes (INF 2/56-74) contain the publicity for various campaigns aimed at the home front, including recruiting campaigns for the army, air force and coal mines.

INF 3 Original Art Work, 1939-1946
1,861 separate pieces of art work commissioned by

d World War

1942	1943	1944	1945

1942	1943	1944	1945
		14 Education Act passed, based on R.A. Butler's White Paper on Education	
CHARNHORST and GNEISENAU ail through the Channel all of Singapore	21 Red Army Day: the King announces presentation of a sword of honour to Stalingrad 28 Bombing raid on Berlin	19 – 26 Heaviest air-raids on London since 1941	4 – 11 Churchill, Roosevelt and Stalin meet at Yalta 14 Allied raid on Dresden
	8 Bethnal Green tube disaster		28 Last of the V rockets falls on London
		– Heavy Allied bombing of Germany and occupied Europe	12 Death of President Roosevelt, succeeded by Harry S. Truman 30 Death of Hitler in Berlin
	7 Montgomery captures Tunis 11 German army in Tunisia surrenders		
		6 D-day landings in Normandy 12 First flying bomb dropped on London	
otion of censure on hurchill debated in ommons after Tobruk oal Commission takes over lliery leases under the oal Act 1938	13 Allied invasion of Sicily	25 Liberation of Paris	17 Beginning of Potsdam conference between Churchill (succeeded by Attlee), Stalin and Truman 27 C.R. Attlee forms Labour government
			6 USA drops atomic bomb on Hiroshima 9 Second atomic bomb dropped on Nagasaki 14 Japan surrenders End of the war
eath of Duke of Kent	3 Italy surrenders	8 First V-2 rockets land on London	
ommel's army defeated at l Alamein	28 (to Dec 1) Meeting between Churchill, Roosevelt and Stalin at Tehran		
Sir William Beveridge's REPORT ON SOCIAL SECURITY published – 23 Battle of Stalingrad		13 Home Guard disbanded	

This is your War

HOME FRONT PROPAGANDA
IN THE SECOND WORLD WAR

London: Her Majesty's Stationery Office

Foreword

This book is one of a series designed by the Public Record Office to make selections from the vast and varied collection of public records more widely available. The series is intended to be of use to teachers of history, political science and social studies in school sixth forms and at universities, polytechnics etc., and to any interested member of the general public.

Her Majesty's Stationery Office

Government Bookshops

49 High Holborn, London WC1V 6HB
13a Castle Street, Edinburgh EH2 3AR
Brazennose Street, Manchester M60 8AS
Southey House, Wine Street, Bristol BS1 2BQ
258 Broad Street, Birmingham B1 2HE
80 Chichester Street, Belfast BT1 4JY

Government publications are also available through booksellers

ISBN 0 11 440166 7
© *Crown copyright 1983*
First published 1983

the Ministry of Information for publicity purposes. Printed versions of much of this material appear in INF 2, but a great deal was not used, so that much of the material in this class is unique and unreproduced. It ranges in size from small drawings to large posters and in medium from pencil to oils, and is arranged, rather confusingly, by both media and themes. The main categories are: oil paintings, caricatures, portraits, posters, drawings for books and booklets, drawings for magazines, war in pictures, political cartoons, publicity for Latin America, war at sea, war on land, war in the air, invasion, general war pictures, empire, 'under Nazi rule', miscellaneous war drawings and Japanese war. Many of the works are unattributed. Artists, where known, include (Sir) Hugh Casson, Terence Cuneo, Fougasse, Ray Illingworth, (Dame) Laura Knight, Mervyn Peake, (Sir) John Piper, Ronald Searle, Strube and Vicky.

INF 4 War of 1914-1918, information services
11 boxes of files and reports on the methods of propaganda used during the First World War.

INF 13 Posters and Publications, 1939-1946
269 collections of printed publicity material issued both by the Ministry of Information and by its successor the Central Office of Information. Much of it is similar to that contained in INF 2.

Ministers of Information during the Second World War

Lord Macmillan	September 1939 – January 1940
Sir John Reith	January 1940 – May 1940
Duff Cooper	May 1940 – July 1941
Brendan Bracken	July 1941 – May 1945
Geoffrey Lloyd	May 1945 – July 1945 (in Churchill's 'caretaker' Conservative government)

Directors General of the Ministry of Information

Sir Kenneth Lee	November 1939 – August 1940
Frank Pick	August 1940 – December 1940
Sir Walter Monckton	December 1940 – December 1941
Sir Cyril Radcliffe	December 1941 – end of war

Introduction

Most government departments after the last war received the honour of an official history. The Ministry of Information (MOI) received merely scorn and derision. Nevertheless the files in its archives tell the story of a remarkable administrative development. From an amateurish coterie concerned primarily with ill-conceived attempts to raise home morale, the Ministry became an efficient organisation for the control and distribution of news and instruction. Its first phase was responsible for its reputation as a laughing stock, vulnerable to satirists like Evelyn Waugh and George Orwell; its second for the less well publicised and moderate guidance of the public in the last half of the war.

A few days before the declaration of war, a Ministry official declared in a memorandum that 'If the Home Front breaks, everything breaks'. Admittedly the urgency of the tone of his note had something to do with the fact that it was a plea to the Treasury for an increase in the funds to be allotted to the Ministry's regional organisation. But the potential importance of the Ministry did rest on the acceptance of the need to strengthen home morale. Its task was not only to give the public information about the war and how to cope with successive crises. It also had to give the government information about public opinion, reactions and behaviour and advise it on how best to unite and strengthen the people. Only gradually was it realised how closely the two functions were linked: the best way to strengthen the war effort was in fact to give the public as much and as frequent news as was compatible with security. Meanwhile, the dual process of informing the public of government decisions and the government of public opinion means that the Ministry's archive gives a very clear picture of the relationship between the people and their leaders. Moreover, the arguments between the Ministry of Information and other departments such as the Treasury, the Foreign Office and the Ministry for Economic Warfare highlight this political question of the need to involve the whole population in the war effort. So that the files – including the often bitter correspondence between ministers – are a valuable political as well as administrative source.

Most directly of all, the documents tell us about life in Britain in the years of the Second World War. Planned in advance but created only in September 1939 and disbanded a few months after VE day, the Ministry reflects the whole story of the British people during these years. A memorandum advising the public how to behave during air raids gives us a valuable description of what the underground shelters

Fig 1   One of a series of posters issued by the Ministry of Health and distributed by the Ministry of Information, which used the slogan 'Coughs and Sneezes Spread Diseases'. Several artists worked on the series. This poster was by H M Bateman. INF 13/188.

1

were like; pamphlets giving background notes for talks by officials throughout the country provide us with detailed information about rationing, factory production and the fears of invasion; posters incidentally illustrate contemporary fashions, the interiors of homes and workshops; regional reports even described the agricultural methods of different parts of the country. Long discussions preceding the production of such memoranda, pamphlets and posters, reported in the minutes of hundreds of committee meetings, give away the assumptions of the policy makers and are an involuntary guide to their attitudes towards various sections of the population such as women or the trades unions. One document can reveal much: the poster illustrated in *fig. 1* shows us not only to what a great extent the Government felt it should encroach on everyday life and its somewhat schoolmasterly attitude to the public; it also tells something of the clothes people wore, the way they did their hair and the atmosphere of the small shop in the high street of the forties before the invasion of the supermarket. The archive is in fact a marvellous source for the social history of the period. Its 944 files, 74 volumes and 136 folders of publicity material and poster campaigns and its 1436 pieces of original art work (listed in the 'Guide to the documents') have been surprisingly little used by the historians – whatever their specialities – of the Second World War.

1. Preparing for the Worst 1936-39. Reassurance

PERSECUTED GERMAN MINORITY

During the First World War a mere 1200 British civilians were killed by German bombs. The people feared and grieved for the men in the trenches but were not frightened for themselves and their young children. The problems of their behaviour and their morale were not sufficiently pressing to demand special attention until 1917, when public support for the war flagged. Then the Government set up a Department (later Ministry) of Information to keep them informed, and a National War Aims Committee (NWAC) to keep them smiling, through the last months of the war. After the armistice, Ministry and NWAC were quickly wound up. The Foreign Office maintained its News Department, and by the mid 1920s several government departments employed press officers, although in practice little seems to have been learned from the short-lived experiment in the First World War. Meanwhile the Government had made some attempt to put its views over to other countries. In 1929 came the Travel Association for encouraging foreigners to come to Britain. Then, largely as an answer to Russian and German efforts at imposing their cultural and political views in the Middle East and Latin America, the British Council emerged in 1934. Three years later the BBC began its foreign language broadcasts. Nevertheless, the government's attitude to any kind of propaganda was suspicious if not outrightly antagonistic. The documents in the Prime Minister's files illustrate this attitude very clearly. When Anthony Eden suggested that some effort should be made to co-ordinate the work of the British Council, the BBC overseas service and the press, Chamberlain's senior adviser Horace Wilson denigrated the

P.M.

   (Having been old-fashioned for very many years, I find myself unable to show enthusiasm for propaganda by this country & I still cannot bring myself to believe that it is a good substitute for calmly getting on with the business of Govt., including a rational foreign policy!)

   Subject to the above, the attached seems on right lines i.e. supervision & co-ordination, provided they don't try to make a great display & ginger-up every agency to fulminate against Italy here & now. Care will be needed in drafting any public announcement. (p.3.) J.H.W. 18.1

Fig 2 Memorandum by Horace Wilson to the Prime Minister, Neville Chamberlain, June 1938.
JHW J Horace Wilson
EH E Hale (Treasury)
PREM 1/272 (*continued overleaf*).

... Hitherto this country has been careful to avoid direct Government propaganda. The British Broadcasting Corporation, the British Council and the Travel Association are all antonomous bodies; and similarly it is intended to deal with the news problem through an independent Reuters. But the Trade Publicity organisation and the National Films Council, having no independent source of income, could have no independent existence. They would be Government Departments. This seems to me to be particularly undesirable in the case of the National Film Council. The original proposal was that the National Film Council should conduct film propaganda at home as well as abroad. I succeeded in getting this, as it seemed to me, most dangerous proposal withdrawn, but once the organisation has been created, its activities could easily be extended to the home front at any time, with results that might be highly undesirable if Government were ever again conducted on party lines.

There is no doubt that the general effect of Government propaganda of recent years has been to poison the international atmosphere. It may be replied that, from that point of view, the measures proposed are at least harmless. I do not believe that any propaganda is really harmless. Even if you are careful, in praising yourself, not to decry others, the unflattering implication is always there. Ten days ago, the British press acclaimed our diplomatic efforts in the cause of peace. That could be read as implying that Germany was on the point of an act of aggression. It was so read in Germany, and bitterly resented. The example is worth quoting as showing how easily the most harmless publicity may give offence. Even apart from this danger, I fear that by entering the propaganda race, we shall intensify it. The appointment of the Vansittart Committee was not unnoticed in Germany, and the announcement of important measures as a result will appear in that country as a challenge. I do not believe that in the long run it will be possible to combine the policy of appeasement with a forward policy in propaganda. Armaments may be infinitely more expensive than propaganda, but they, at least, have the virtue of being dumb, and do not cause the same ill-will. From the point of view of appeasement, the propaganda race seems to me to be the more serious danger.

E.H.
2/6/38

whole idea of propaganda[1] (*fig. 2*). A Treasury representative did not see how anti-fascist propaganda could be combined with a policy of appeasement.

Fig 2a Summary of Sir R Vansittart's proposals on 'Publicity Abroad' made by E. Hale. PREM 1/272.

[1]PREM 1/272

By this time it had been admitted that in the event of war it would be necessary to establish some organisation for putting the government's point of view at home as well as abroad. Through his propaganda ministry, Goebbels was using the press, radio, exhibitions, posters, the theatre and especially the cinema to create the Fuhrer legend and promote the cause of Nazism. If war came, the German people would be easily manipulated by their leaders. But what about the British? This time they would not only be in the front line because of the extended range of the bombers; the demands of the new technological warfare would involve them all in its prosecution. So in October 1935 a sub-committee of the Committee of Imperial Defence (CID) chaired by John Colville was appointed 'to prepare plans for the establishment on the outbreak of war of a Ministry of Information'.[2] In July it issued its report setting out the proposed functions and structure of the new Ministry under the recommended Director Generalship of Stephen Tallents from the BBC.[3] The tasks of the Ministry were to disseminate news, take responsibility for censorship of the media and 'present the public cause' at home and abroad.

Propaganda in enemy countries was later given to the Political Warfare Executive under Hugh Dalton. At home the publicity division officials clearly saw part of their role as morale raising. In a report prepared in September 1938 they summed up their task as the dissemination of instructions, appeals and advice of government departments, to 'prevent panic, allay misapprehensions' and 'generally to keep the public in good heart'.[4] But with little enthusiasm from the politicians and little direction from the top of the embryo Ministry, no coherent philosophy of propaganda had emerged by the outbreak of war. There was little co-ordinated discussion about how these aims should be carried out. One of the few suggestions agreed to be 'valuable' was the provision of tea to allay panic after air raids. Nor was recruitment to the Ministry designed to help constructive propaganda planning. Many of the new men were academics, career civil servants like the Deputy Director General, A.P. Waterfield, or men well known for their strong individual views like film producer Sydney Bernstein, Joseph Ball who also later became a film producer, or the poet John Betjeman. None had a training in psychology, and few had the kind of background which might have given them a better understanding of how most people lived. Officials were sensitive to implied criticism in the unsolicited advice received from academic psychologists. Waterfield thought that a letter from an Edinburgh professor early in 1940 merely 'cracks up his own department and tells (us) that ours is rotten'; and in September 1941 the suggestion of an advisory committee of psychologists was greeted with horror by R.H. Parker, Director of the Home Division.[5]

It is clear from the recommendations filling the early documents that the men from the Ministry under-estimated the resilience of the British people to face the impact of Hitler. One internal memorandum warned: 'The Ministry must prepare for the worst, that is to assume that the public may be subjected to an appalling series of shocks, the effect of

[2]CAB 16/127 [3]PREM 1/388 CID 1253-B [4]INF 1/713 [5]INF 1/318

which . . . may be that nerves will be shattered and . . . the will to victory be grievously impaired'.[6] Their aim was therefore to strengthen the resolve of a weak people. In April 1940 the publicity division considered 'our basic propaganda theme must be that victory is certain if the nation "sticks it out" '.[7] The public must be encouraged to expect, face and then ignore early setbacks. The tone of the campaign should be 'restraint and sober determination'. Waterfield's draft speech for the King, sent to the Home Secretary for approval but never broadcast, called on 'my people to stand calm and firm in this time of trial'.[8] A possible slogan might be 'We're going to see it through'. In May came a suggestion for the design of the first poster: over the caption 'stand firm: strike hard for freedom', a longbowman of the Hundred Years' War stood with his feet firmly planted on a map of England. In a secret memorandum on propaganda it was pointed out that 'trappings and pageantry inherited from the past' formed valuable propaganda for stability.[9]

The official in charge of Home Publicity research thought that even this design was asking too much of the British: they could not be expected to respond to abstract academic concepts like freedom. An attitude would be easier to grasp: 'What is surely needed first is to promote an attitude of cheerful courage in keeping with the British character'.[10] The argument was accepted by his colleagues. Waterfield produced the caption '*Your* courage, *your* cheerfulness, *your* resolution will bring us victory'.[11] The previous month, when the campaign material from the last war had been found, the Home Publicity division had expressly warned against repeating the mistake of captions with 'the implied distinction between *you* and *we*'. Nevertheless, Waterfield's words were blown up and the offending pronouns underlined on the early poster. *The Times* called it 'an insipid and patronising invocation'. The attitude reappeared in the equally uninspiring poster of Beaverbrook and Harriman encouraging increased arms production for their new ally[12] (*fig. 3*).

The minutes and memoranda of the early ministerial committees make it clear that there was a distinction between government and governed in the minds of their members. One of the chief aims to the Ministry's propaganda was to persuade the people that every one of them must feel involved in what was bound to be a total war. Hence the emphasis on the second person in slogans and the tone of pamphlets like 'How *you* can help'. The longbowman in the poster was clearly drawn to show he was a member of the lower orders, implying the involvement of everyman in the war effort. Yet officials and their propaganda betrayed a lack of confidence in the public. A memorandum to the Director of Home Publicity early in September emphasised that the language of the BBC must be kept simple and homely because the vast majority of the population left school at fourteen or under: phrases like 'transport' or 'congested areas' should be avoided. Intellectuals and

[6]INF 1/299   [7]INF 1/727   [8]INF 1/670   [9]INF 1/724   [10]INF 1/723
[11]INF 1/226   [12]INF 13/123

We have pledged your faith, the faith of the men and women of Britain. You must do the deed . . . **STALIN MUST BE SUSTAINED**

Lord Beaverbrook

Averell Harriman

RUSH AID TO RUSSIA!

writers called in to produce publicity material did nothing to modify the view of the public held by Ministry officials. A.A. Milne, used to creating fantasies for children, produced a draft speech to be broadcast by the Queen[13] (*fig. 4*). It was an insult to the intelligence of the public – or certainly of women, to whom it was addressed; but the Director General found it 'generally admirable'. The idea of the broadcast, however, was eventually rejected.

The academics and civil servants in the Ministry tended to believe that the public were unable to understand or cope with the crisis. In their view, people had to be encouraged to be brave, resolute and cheerful. No co-ordinated system of intelligence existed to prove their view wrong, to report the real attitudes and resilience of the nation. Waterfield was aware of the deficiency.[14] He told the Treasury that John Beresford, head of the collecting division, was unhappy with his low budget; he would like to contact organisations such as the British Institute of Public Opinion used by the *News Chronicle*, or Mass Observation set up by Tom Harrisson in 1937 to produce surveys of public opinion.

Lack of a good intelligence system meant a gap in understanding between government and governed; and this understanding was a necessary condition of effective propaganda. Not only research but vital forward planning was curtailed by Treasury veto. If the Ministry was forbidden to rent commercial sites in advance of hostilities, their poster campaign was unlikely to make much immediate impact.[15] When war came, however, the new Ministry was physically ready. Regional information offices and local information committees had been planned

Fig 3 One of a series of posters issued in support of the alliance between Great Britain, the USA and the Soviet Union. This one appeared after Lord Beaverbrook and the US envoy Averell Harriman had visited Moscow to arrange for the supply of war material to Russia. INF 13/123.

[13]INF 1/670 [14]INF 1/329 [15]INF 1/723

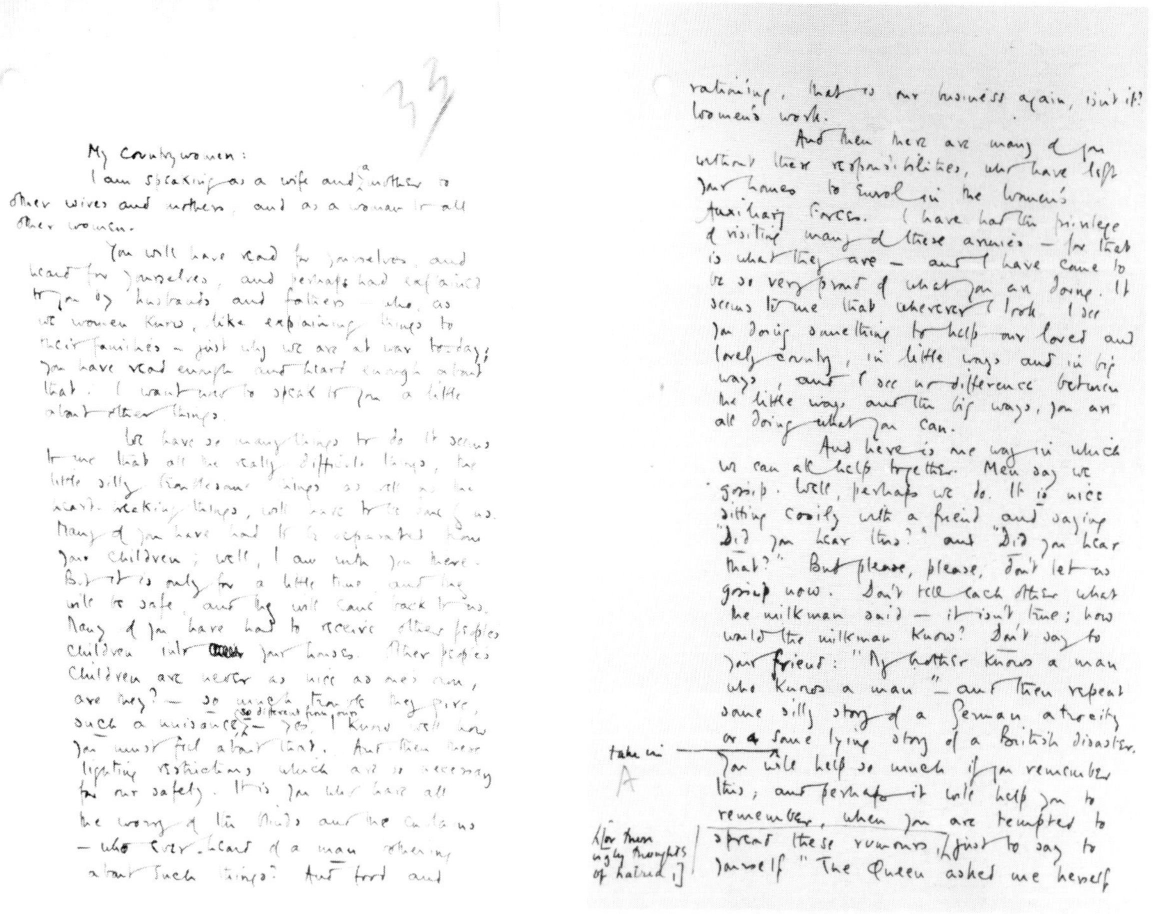

for all areas.[16] Waterfield told the Home Secretary on 30 August that the censorship and news divisions were ready to go into action.[17] All was prepared for smoothly transferring the BBC to the Ministry.[18] The first posters were designed, the first pamphlets written. Every division knew where its office would be: news and censorship, the policy and administrative divisions were all in Senate House; home publicity at 32 Chesham Place and foreign publicity at 38 Belgrave Square. Outwardly the Ministry of Information was well organised. But it still had to learn the art of propaganda.

Fig 4   Address to British women, drafted by A A Milne for the Queen to broadcast in 1939. It was not used. INF 1/670.

[16]INF 1/294-5   [17]INF 1/852   [18]INF 1/869

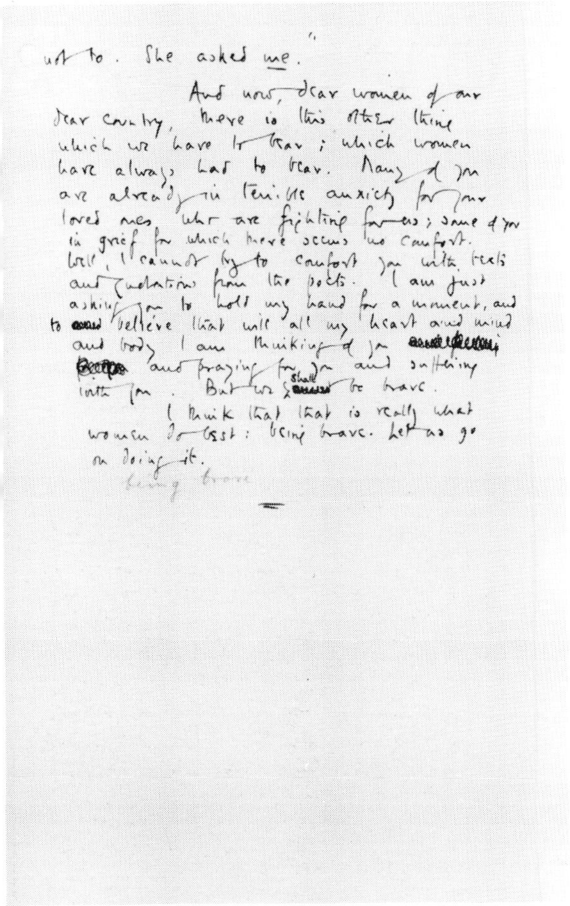

...t to. She asked me."

And now, dear women of our dear country, there is this other thing which we have to bear; which women have always had to bear. Many of you are already in terrible anxiety for your loved ones, who are fighting for us; some of you in grief for which there seems no comfort. Well, I cannot try to comfort you with texts and quotations from the poets. I am just asking you to hold my hand for a moment, and to ~~now~~ believe that with all my heart and mind and body I am thinking of you ~~and every~~ ~~today~~ and praying for you and suffering with you. But we shall be brave.

I think that that is really what women do best: being brave. Let us go on doing it.

being brave

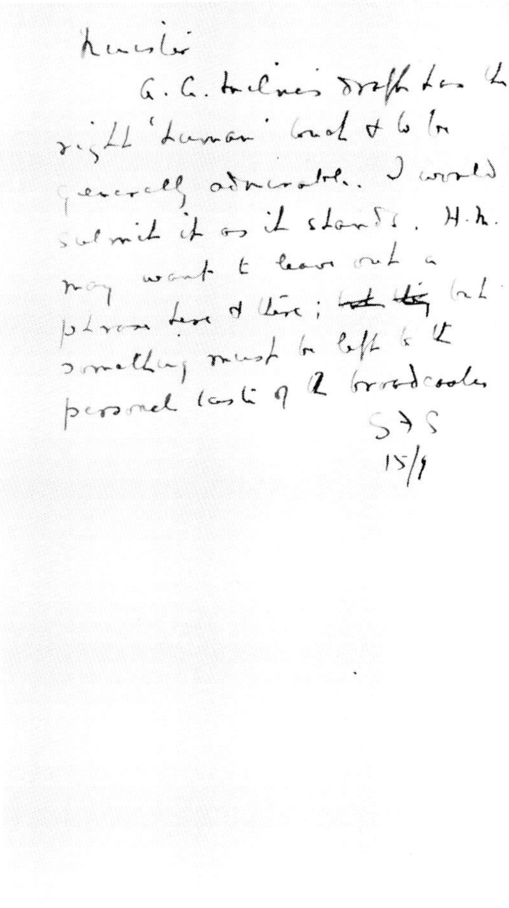

Director

A. A. Milne's draft has the right 'human' touch & to be generally admirable. I would submit it as it stands. H.H. may want to leave out a phrase here & there; ~~but they~~ but something must be left to the personal taste of the broadcaster

S.J.S
15/1

ARYAN TYPE

2. The Phoney War
September 1939-April 1940:
Exhortation

The first air raid warning sounded at 11.20 on 3 September 1939. It was another year before the bombing began in earnest. So that while the war at sea was waged bitterly from the first, nothing drastic happened at once to disturb civilian life. The task of the Ministry of Information, formally given birth on the declaration of war, was to monitor and guide this civilian life. But Lord Macmillan, the new minister, and his officials like everyone else misjudged the situation. They saw their first task as keeping the public resolute in face of an immediate onslaught.

Four million copies of three posters were produced for the hoardings by the end of September.[19] Their messages were 'Keep Calm and Carry on', Waterfield's 'Your courage, your cheerfulness, will bring us victory' and – a little more aggressively – 'Freedom is in Peril: Defend it with all your might'.[20] Although the picture palaces so popular during the thirties were closed down on 3 September it was soon considered advisable to open them, both as an important propaganda medium and as a means of alleviating the depression caused each evening by the blackout. In the films section of the publicity division it was decided that the features most suitable for showing were 'The Lady Vanishes' and 'Mr Chips': they brought out the required qualities of calmness in crisis and acceptance of adversity.[21] Such virtues should also be evident in the five-minute films and longer documentaries commissioned either from independent producers or from the Crown Film Unit taken over from the General Post Office (GPO) by the Ministry. An obligatory quota of these films was taken by every local cinema.

Pamphlets with titles like 'The Struggle Ahead' also emphasised the grit and determination expected of the public.[22] The second batch of posters designed by the publicity division showed representatives of the three Services in a series captioned 'The Empire's Strength';[23] and under the heading 'Britain's War Effort' a ship builder, a coal miner, a munitions worker or a land girl were shown hard at work at their respective tasks. Individual artists were commissioned to produce these designs. On 31 October, R.A. Bevan, the head of Home Publicity General Production, wrote to the well-known artist Dame Laura Knight 'about doing a pictorial poster, and the subject which it was suggested you might like to do was the Women's Land Army, as part of a series illustrating Britain's war effort'.[24] Bevan explained that the Ministry offered ten guineas for a preliminary sketch and 'Seventy

Fig 5   Poster issued soon after war was declared. INF 13/218.

[19]INF 1/302   [20]INF 13/213   [21]INF 1/252   [22]INF 1/724   [23]INF 2/231
[24]INF 1/637

GAS ATTACK

HOW TO PUT ON YOUR GAS MASK

Always keep your gas mask with you — day and night. Learn to put it on quickly. Practise wearing it.

1. Hold your breath. 2. Hold mask in front of face, with thumbs inside straps.
3. Thrust chin well forward into mask, pull straps over head as far as they will go.
4. Run finger round face-piece taking care head-straps are not twisted.

IF THE GAS RATTLES SOUND

1. Hold your breath. Put on mask wherever you are. Close window.

2. If out of doors, take off hat, put on your mask. Turn up collar.

3. Put on gloves or keep hands in pockets. Take cover in nearest building.

IF YOU GET GASSED

BY VAPOUR GAS	Keep your gas mask on even if you feel discomfort. If discomfort continues go to First Aid Post

BY LIQUID or BLISTER GAS

1	2	3	4
Dab, but *don't rub* the splash with handkerchief. Then destroy handkerchief.	Rub No. 2 Ointment well into place. *(Buy a 6d. jar now from any chemist).* In emergency chemists supply Bleach Cream free.	If you can't get Ointment or Cream within 5 minutes wash place with soap and warm water	Take off at once any garment splashed with gas.

11

guineas for the rough sketches and the finished design'. After several letters and a refusal to present a preliminary sketch, Dame Laura won permission to produce the poster on her own terms.

While persuading the public they were in the stable hands of the military and the industrial workers, the Ministry officials had to prepare them for the expected attack. Committee meeting minutes for the publicity division of 5 September 1939 reported that a five-minute film on how to put on a gas mask was ready for distribution.[25] A poster was produced with the same instructions[26] (*fig. 5*). Its spelling out of the simple stages of the operation was typical of the Ministry's estimation of the intelligence of the public. The only change from the pre-war discussions about the best way of preventing panic during air raids was in the recommendation of coffee rather than tea: 'Scared people sheltering during a raid should be made to sit quietly, be told their fear is only natural and given a cup of coffee after which they should be all right'. It is not surprising that the Home Office, shown a copy of this memorandum of 13 September on 'The Preservation of Civilian Morale' considered it 'rather childish' and that 'it greatly undervalues the spirit of our people'.[27]

Officials necessarily spent much time and effort putting out pre-cautionary material whose message was hardly cheerful. Inundating the public with leaflets and posters forbidding them to show any light at night, warning them – in Cyril Kenneth Bird's 'Fougasse' cartoons – that 'Careless talk costs lives', and instructing them to send their children away from the towns, it was perhaps understandable that they should imagine public morale to be very low. Their first experimental use of Mass Observation in October 1939 told them that the public not only criticised the posters begging them to defend freedom as too abstract, but were encouraged by them to wonder whether the government's regulations or Hitler were depriving them of more freedom.[28] Also resented was the implication in Waterfield's 'cheerfulness and courage' caption that the public were expected to fight the war for the government's benefit. Apart from this isolated enquiry the Ministry had as yet no research facilities for measuring the morale of the public or its reactions to its campaigns. At the end of January 1940 Mary Adams was brought over from the BBC to set up a Home Intelligence Unit. But until it began to function efficiently the Ministry still had no organised method of discovering that the morale of the people was in fact far higher than it imagined.

Perhaps another reason why the Ministry officials underestimated public morale was that their own was not too high. The energy of the Ministry during the first few months was wasted in a dispute with the Services over the control of news and censorship. A letter in the ministerial 'propaganda policy' file shows Waterfield complaining to the War Office just one day after the declaration of war that 'the arrangements which have been made for the centralisation of the

[25]INF 1/302 [26]INF 13/218 [27]HO 199/434 [28]INF 1/261

supply of all information to the public through the Ministry failed to work yesterday'.[29] News of the appointment of Generals Lord Gort and Edmund Ironside had been given direct to the BBC by the War Office without going through the Ministry. More friction came the next day when the Air Ministry similarly bypassed the MOI. Not to be outdone, on day three of the war the Admiralty put out an announcement of the sinking of German ships without first getting clearance from Macmillan's officials. Already the prestige of the new Ministry was low. By 16 September, after repeated discussions in various committees about the rights and responsibilities of the Ministry, Waterfield drew up a draft memorandum to be circulated to the Cabinet in Macmillan's name: 'My experience in the short time since I took up office has convinced me that if the MOI is to play the part which has been laid down for it . . . there must be a fundamental change in the relations between it and the Departments of State which are mainly responsible for the conduct of the war'.

The first draft of the memorandum had complained that the Ministry was 'on the way to becoming a laughing stock'. There is no doubt that the officials from Macmillan downwards felt insecure. They were criticised in the House of Lords for ineptitude and overstaffing, slated in the *New Statesman* for nepotism and satirised by Tommy Handley on the BBC as the Ministry of Aggravation. Macmillan admitted in the Lords when his Ministry was under fire that he had 'had considerable difficulty in ascertaining its function'.[30] One function he soon had no need to bother about. For the Cabinet took no heed either of his memorandum or of John Beresford's plea for a central news department. Instead, on 3 October, the Prime Minister announced that an independent News and Censorship Board would take over these functions from the Ministry. An Air Ministry paper of 7 October trying to draw a distinction between news – to be dealt with by the service departments on the authority of the new Board – and publicity as the responsibility of the MOI, shows the impracticability of the new arrangement. Waterfield claimed that such a division 'in the face of the immense advantage which the Germans enjoy through their vast propaganda machine, with its penetrating activities and its unity of control . . . would appear to be sheer lunacy'.[31]

Nor was the chairman of the Press and Censorship Board, Walter Monckton, at all happy about his position. After a month of little co-operation from the Services he wrote to Horace Wilson saying that the Board could not survive without radical change.[32] A letter on the same file dated a fortnight later shows him threatening his resignation to Home Secretary John Anderson unless he is given 'the last word except where the message is of vital importance to the Services'. Sixty-seven Ministry officials and several regional officers had lost their jobs; Chamberlain was even reported to be thinking of winding up the whole department. But Monckton's troubles persuaded the Cabinet to try to strengthen the Ministry instead of destroying it: in January 1940

---

[29]INF 1/852   [30]Hansard series V vol.114, col.1129   [31]INF 1/853   [32]INF 1/854

Macmillan was replaced by John Reith who had imposed his high moral standards on British broadcasting since 1922: and in April the Press and Censorship Board was reabsorbed by the Ministry with Monckton as Assistant Director General.

Meanwhile the officials were beginning to realise that their emphasis on reassuring the public might be misplaced. The people were not panicking. Encouragement to 'keep calm' seemed as unnecessary as instructions about blackout and gasmasks – and as boring. During the long 'Phoney War' apathy, not panic, was in the air. It particularly affected both the evacuees and their harrassed hosts. Complaints from both were regular features of the Home Intelligence weekly reports.[33] The Home Publicity division decided in November 1939 that the posters of terrified children huddling together as the bombs fell, over a caption begging Mother to send them to safety, were irrelevant in the raid-free cities. They were replaced by Mother tempted by a Hitler figure to bring her offspring home[34] (fig. 6). For many of the thousands who had responded in the first few days of the war to the early posters and to the Ministry inspired articles about happy refugees written by Godfrey Winn for the women's journals, had begun to trickle back to the towns for Christmas at home.[35]

All sense of an urgent need to keep steady and cheerful had disappeared. The Committee minutes of the planning section of the publicity division show that on 5 January 1940 – the day Reith took over from Macmillan – a change of attitude was considered essential: 'Reassurance should now give way to arousing the public from complacency.'[36] Leaflets and museum exhibitions should involve people in the war effort. The following week the committee heard Mary Adams outline a plan for various exhibitions to travel around the country and be shown in stores and government offices with the aim of 'replacing public bewilderment with a strong sense of what they were fighting for'. In a long memorandum the new Minister in February warned a Cabinet committee that if apathy and boredom continued, pacifism would grow: 'Among the less informed classes a passive, negative feeling of apathy and boredom is apparent . . . There is a general feeling that individuals do not count in the conduct of the war and that the only thing to do is to live as normal a life as possible'[37] Reith's policy committee were told that 'a time of stagnation needs most effort'. On his instructions they drafted a paper for Cabinet advocating 'a call to arms, to effort to self-sacrifice'. The message to the public should be 'This is your war, the nation's war. You decided rightly, that it had to come. You wage it; no one else can. You will end it; for it can't be fought without you'.[38]

Various methods were discussed for pulling people out of their apathy. Kenneth Clark, in his new role of controller of production, reported that of the 32 films made by the film division during the first

[33]INF 1/292   [34]INF 13/171   [35]INF 1/302   [36]INF 1/316   [37]INF 1/867
[38]INF 1/848

Fig 6   Poster designed to support the evacuation of children from the cities, 1939. INF 13/171.

15

two months of 1940, some had been designed to reassure, others to prevent apathy[39] (*fig. 7*).

Note for inclusion in General Report to the Cabinet

FILM DIVISION

Since January the Division has commissioned thirty-two films showing various aspects of our part in the war. Some of these are intended to reassure, others to prevent apathy; a certain number are designed primarily for foreign or Empire distribution. Three of these films are already completed; most of the remainder will be released in the course of a month. The Division has also put into production three short dramatic films showing the tragic effects of gossip. These will be released early in March. As a result of active co-operation the selection and quality of newsreel material has improved. The Director is in close touch with the heads of all the big producing companies in this country, both British and American, and has persuaded nearly all of them to produce films which present our war aims and effort in a favourable light.

21st February 1940.

An imperious Britannia looked down from many hoardings remarking 'It's up to You',[40] (*fig. 8*) while from others Churchill quoted his own exhortations: 'Let us Go Forward Together'.[41] The publicity division decided that a leaflet encouraging the public to greater involvement in the war effort could, with the co-operation of the book clubs, be inserted in every volume sold by them. Assistant Director General Ivison Macadam asked novelist Hugh Walpole to produce a suitable text for the leaflet. Walpole had written to Macmillan at the outbreak of war congratulating him on his appointment and offering his services.[42] He had been in Beaverbrook's Ministry of Information in 1918 and was now involved in the abortive attempt by the Ministry to form a committee of authors to advise the department on publications. By December 1939 it had become clear that the differing interests of the publishers led by Geoffrey Faber and literary agents represented by A.D. Peters, to say nothing of the idiosyncrasies of individual authors, would make such a committee impossible. So Walpole was free to write Macadam's pamphlet. R.A. Bevan's reaction after the text had been lost in the post and recovered, was 'not very favourable'.[43] Another official thought it smug and 'more highbrow than I had expected' but recommended distribution. His criticism was justified: 'The Freedom of Books', as the pamphlet was called, praised British democracy as a way of life; it called to witness Shelley, Milton, Bunyan, Samuel Johnson,

Fig 7   Note to be included in General Report to the Cabinet February 1940. INF 1/3

[39]INF 1/3   [40]INF 3/129   [41]INF 13/213

Tom Jones, Mr Pickwick, Mark Rutherford, Mr Polly, Thackeray, Charles Kingsley, Pope, Cromwell and Pym amongst others by whom many book club readers must have been unimpressed.

Just as literary and as unsuitable as Walpole's leaflet were some of the posters pasted across the country's hoardings. 'Government of the People by the People for the People shall not perish from the earth' made no immediate impact.[44] More succinct but almost as uncolloquial was 'Mightier Yet' written in enormous letters beneath a sturdy British battleship; and later encouragements to collect salvage presumed a knowledge of Shakespeare and Dumas: 'The Three Salvageers' were shown collecting bones, paper and metal, while on others they asked 'When Shall We Three Meet Again?'[45] (*fig. 9*). A similar obscurity bedevilled the campaign of the Empire section of the publicity division: its ponderous language failed to arouse any enthusiasm for the democratic way of life of the British Commonwealth.[46]

By April 1940 the Ministry had recovered a little from its early reputation. Once again it was responsible for news and censorship; the local committees had revived to the extent that 200 public meetings were taking place every week; the Intelligence unit was ready; by March the Ministry had established its claim, at least in theory, to veto BBC programmes[47] (*fig. 14*). But the squabbles with the Services over censorship and with the publishers over the committee of authors had wasted energy. An early anti-waste campaign was ill organised and amateurish, largely due to an inability to divide responsibility between departments.[48] Most of these failures could be traced to a weakness in personnel. Reith did create a more aggressive image for the Ministry than his ineffectual predecessor. But he, too, failed to assert the authority of the MOI. Nor were the successive Directors General more suited to their task. Neither Findlater Stewart, the civil servant seconded from the India Office, nor Kenneth Lee, an ex-chief engineer at the GPO, had the most appropriate talents or experience for guiding the public. Lee was criticised by Reith in his diary entry of 26 March, 1940 as 'utterly ineffective'. Not much more could be said of the Ministry's attempts in these first few months either at reassuring or inspiring the people.

IT'S UP TO YOU

[42]INF 1/229   [43]INF 1/227   [44]INF 1/316   [45]INF 13/148   [46]INF 1/251
[47]INF 1/168   [48]INF 1/340

Fig 8   Preliminary sketch for a poster by Tom Purvis. INF 3/129.

Fig 9   Poster by Strube in the salvage
campaign series. INF 13/148 part 1.

3. Dunkirk May-August 1940: Suspicion

TECHNICAL EXPERT

Churchill's arrival in Downing Street did not immediately sweep a different breed of men into Senate House. The new Director General, Frank Pick (whose history included the London Passenger Transport Board and the Council for Art and Industry) was probably more efficient but no more imaginative than his predecessor. According to Monckton, he spent too much time ratifying expenditure and too little discussing the principles of propaganda.[49] Duff Cooper who might have expected more from Churchill after his resignation from the Admiralty over Munich, was the new minister. He and his Parliamentary Secretary, Harold Nicolson, were only too willing to discuss principles, probably over the lunch tables of society hostesses. Their education and experience had given them few contacts with the people whose morale was now their responsibility. Nor was their own morale high after the German invasion of Belgium. Nicolson told his wife, Vita Sackville West, to have 'a bare bodkin handy so that you can take your quietus when necessary. I shall have one also'.[50]

It was in this frame of mind that Nicolson, with Kenneth Clark and Ivison Macadam, was entrusted by the Policy Committee 'with the task of examining methods to maintain public morale during the days of stress and danger' ahead.[51] Their first recommendations were less impressive than their title of Home Morale Emergency Committee: the public should be made more aware of Air Raid Precaution (ARP) facilities; actors should lead sing-songs in the shelters and Boy Scouts should look out for alien parachutists. Posters were even produced illustrating the uniforms of German parachutists and servicemen so that the public could 'spot them on sight'.[52] Equally suitable for a *Boys' Own* adventure story was a five-minute documentary showing the public how to use church bells as an alarm signal and how to alert the Local Defence Volunteers, later known as the Home Guard, if they saw invaders approaching.[53] Rather more useful was another short on the ARP suggested by John Betjeman in the films division.[54]

The successful evacuation of Dunkirk avoided the annihilation of the British Expeditionary Force (BEF) but brought nearer the threat of invasion. It was now felt, the Emergency Committee reported in a memorandum to the policy committee, 'that what the public now desired was not so much exhortation as guidance, not so much words of

[49]INF 1/253
[50]Nigel Nicolson (ed.) *Diaries and Letters of Harold Nicolson 1939-45*, entry for 26 May 1940
[51]INF 1/250   [52]INF 13/213   [53]INF 1/208   [54]INF 1/206

comfort as words of command'.[55] But how much guidance did the Ministry actually give to the public? Admittedly, they had little assistance from the Ministry of Home Security or the War Office. It was left to the Emergency Committee in June to draft the pamphlet laying down the rules for the British should the invaders come. If they found themselves behind enemy lines they were told to make the German position difficult. On the other hand they were given no guidance as to how far they could take aggressive or even defensive measures. Duff Cooper tried in vain to make the Cabinet issue a firm directive to the public.[56] After the Ministry of Home Security had even objected to the MOI suggestion that people should be encouraged to dig trenches,[57] Cooper in despair asked Attlee: 'Are we to encourage women to throw Molotoff cocktails out of the window on advancing troops or tanks and are we to encourage those who have the necessary knowledge to use a rifle? Frankly I am not clear what the Government's policy is on this. Are you?'[58] The cocktails were the idea of the Women's Voluntary Service.

France fell on 17 June 1940. Just as Reith and Mary Adams had exaggerated the danger of apathy producing pacifism, so now Duff Cooper and his officials believed the growing fear of invasion would lead to defeatism. Committee minutes of the Emergency Committee reported agreement on 'The importance of combatting the idea that we could reach a reasonable peace with Germany'.[59] Regional officers reported a few remarks about how little difference it would make to have to pay taxes to Hitler rather than to the Government.[60] Probably for want of anything more interesting to include in their weekly bulletins they commented on the numbers of pacifists, communists and Jews – however few – at local meetings. Wary official eyes were kept on left-wing pacifist journals.[61] There was little evidence that such fears were justified or pacifism growing. Yet pamphlets spelling out 'What Would Happen if Hitler Won' warned the public that German peace terms would mean 'you couldn't make a joke in the pub without being afraid that a spy might not get you run in or beaten up; you couldn't talk freely in front of your children for fear that they might give you away (in Germany they are encouraged to)'.[62] Notes for speakers to be circulated to the Local Information Officers on 'What the German Occupation Means' prophesied the moral and economic exploitation of the public. Anti-pacifist propaganda was fed to the press.[63]

A Home Intelligence memorandum written the day France fell illustrates official fears of public defeatism[64] (*fig. 10*). Potential quislings were seen everywhere. Duff Cooper had no qualms about his government's policy in introducing the 18b regulation allowing aliens to be restricted or imprisoned. In fact, the daily reports of the Home Intelligence unit during June and July showed few signs of dis-affection.[65] But just how seriously the Ministry feared traitors is

[55]INF 1/252 [56]CAB 66/8. WP (40) 190 [57]INF 1/878 [58]INF 1/258
[59]INF 1/249 [60]INF 1/257 [61]INF 1/319 [62]INF 1/332 [63]INF 1/319
[64]INF 1/257 [65]INF 1/846

Reference _____

To: R. B. Stevens

From: C. H. Wilson.

In view of the extremely widespread distribution of rumours that the British Government is preparing to leave for Canada, I consider that some positive counter-statement by the Government is urgently desirable.

These rumours take many different forms. Some suggest that the Government is contemplating flight to Canada as soon as invasion starts, while others, without going to such extremes, suggest that a shadow Cabinet is already being formed the other side of the Atlantic. Further rumours about the imminent departure of the Royal Family and reports that the Royal Princesses have already left help to strengthen these ideas.

[Linked up with these is another aspect of present public opinion. People are saying that they wouldn't be much worse off under Hitler, and with their own leaders likely to run away they might as well accept the inevitable.]

The absence of any official statement as to the Government's intentions lends support to these rumours, which are producing a general attitude of defeatism among wide sections of the public. This might easily pass into panic if the situation worsened rapidly.

Charles H. Wilson.

[handwritten] Today, Home Intelligence report says that rumours are current in 20 States.

17th June, 1940.

W135500/1128
2,500M 12/39 FHD
51-5418
(REGIMITE)

[handwritten] The French surrender makes some statement, such as that suggested by Mr Wilson in his first sentence, more desirable even than before. I understand that Marshal Pétain said it would be unfair to the French people & the Govt. moved to North Africa etc. RBS. 17/6
Mr Leigh Ashton

[margin handwritten] See separate minute / my taxi driver said How's me this morning J.A.

---

obvious from the pamphlet produced by Kenneth Clark and Ivison Macadam on 'Fifth Column Tricks'. It warned the public that the enemy would arrive by parachute or small boat disguised as nuns, clergymen, ARP workers or Boy Scouts; they would wreck communications, seize railway stations and banks, kidnap Cabinet Ministers and members of the royal family and initiate rumours.[66] Waterfield had the sense to realise that such a leaflet might possibly cause panic. But Kenneth Clark agreed with his view that 'a well written pamphlet dealing with this subject in a balanced way is badly needed, despite the fact that it may give some foundation to a crop of rumours'.[67]

Waterfield and Clark were wrong: the publicity about fifth columnists

Fig 10   Memorandum by the Home Intelligence Department of the Ministry of Information, on low morale in June 1940.

L A Leigh Ashton
RBS R B Stevens
INF 1/257

[66]INF 1/249   [67]INF 1/333

Dear Sir,

I am amazed at the way people are talking of late. I work in one of the biggest armaments factory and on all sides of me I hear discussions going on. I cannot put into words what they say about the BBC, and any opposition I make to what they say, they call me alsorts of fools for believing you, and I find that nine out of every ten of them listen to Lord Haw-Haw, saying they can get more truth from him, and they want me to do the same. They are saying that this terrible defeat in Flanders, is being twisted into a victory. It is a standing joke in the factory about your oft repeated phrase, 'all our planes returned safely'. According to them the govenment ought to be shot for what they have done to our boys, and though I dont know what they mean they say the Mayfair clique are leading our men to their doom. They said to me to-day for instance, how crafty they are in trying to camouflage Lord Gorts return here into something noble, they say that the stuttering officer who spoke in Gorts defence, was an example of the type of men who are leading us to-day. Really I am so bewildered by all they say that I do not know what to believe, am I to believe that Germany have got us in a trap like they say. I feel I must listen to German news now, or I cannot argue unless I know the two sides.

Yours Truly

Miss Verney

aroused public fears of invasion without giving any useful advice. Anyone behaving at all unusually was suspect – including the actors making 'Fires were Started' for the film division of the Ministry.[68] More important, the half expected crop of rumours indeed appeared. Bred by the fear of invasion, alarmist stories of German plans had increased since France fell. German radio propaganda cleverly exaggerated the suspicions and rumours. William Joyce, known as Lord Haw-Haw because of his accent, was regularly cited – in letters from the public to the Ministry – as the source of these stories: Bradford Grammar School would be used as the headquarters of the Reichstag;[69] a regiment had been wiped out at Winchester and British ships sunk in home harbours by German bombs.[70] The welfare of British soldiers was being neglected by their generals and British policy being run for the benefit of a 'Mayfair clique'[71] (fig. 11).

Most popular were the stories of invasion and the concurrent rumour that this 'clique', the government, was planning to take itself off to Canada[72] (fig. 10). Three Home Intelligence files contain letters asking for confirmation that certain towns were to expect raids on certain days; other letters blamed colleagues at work or wives' 'tittle-tattle' for spreading alarmist stories.[73]

Fig 11 Letter to the Ministry of Information from a member of the public, quoting rumours. INF 1/266.

Fig 12 A poster in the campaign against gossip, 1940. INF 13/216.

[68]INF 1/212 [69]INF 1/263 [70]INF 1/266 [71]INF 1/266 [72]INF 1/267,257 [73]INF 1/265

Obviously the Ministry had to do something about the growing habit of rumour mongering. Monitoring of foreign broadcasts quickly exonerated Lord Haw-Haw from blame for most of the stories so there was no point in banning them. BBC talks by Priestley and others had some effect. The campaign against 'Careless Talk' had been one of the first planned by the Ministry. The Fougasse posters were designed for the railways in November 1939 and were not – as many writers assumed before the MOI archives were opened – a response to Haw-Haw. They were light-hearted, emphasising the gossiping housewives rather than the more comic menacing Nazis who could overhear them in the bus or cafe. The following series appealed in matter of fact terms to a responsible public, showing a plane brought down or a ship sunk as the result of an indiscreet confidence[74] (*fig. 12*).

But on 5 July 1940 Kenneth Clark told the Policy Committee that Churchill had given instructions for a wide campaign to be put in hand immediately against the dangers of rumours. 'Confusing rumours' would now be added to the themes of 'dangerous gossip' and 'defeatist talk'.[75] Harold Nicolson agreed that the Ministry's present methods were not nearly intensive enough. The following two weeks dangerous citizens like Miss Leaky Mouth, Miss Teacup Whisper and Mr Pride in Prophesy stared out malevolently from the press and hoardings. The public were told to 'Join Britain's silent column – the great body of sensible men and women who have pledged themselves not to rumour and gossip and to stop others doing it'. The last phrase encouraged them to inform on the rumour mongers. Not many did so; but the campaign naturally provoked suspicion among acquaintances and colleagues. The Home Intelligence report of 16 July commented: 'There is evidence that the Silent Column campaign, although receiving public response, is not having a desirable psychological effect. Social workers and observers report increasing suspicion and unneighbourliness'.[76] Macadam and Kenneth Clark agreed it might be better to encourage people rather than scare them out of their wits.[77] In the Policy Committee of 23 July it was generally felt that the campaign had been unlucky and that the offending phrase 'the silent column' should be gradually abandoned.[78] Once again the anti-gossip campaign became gentler in approach. 'Be like Dad, keep Mum' was adopted as a less provocative slogan in spite of Edith Summerskill's objection that it was in bad taste.[79] The new 'soft-sell' approach even used a sexual angle[80] (*fig. 13*). Minutes of the Home Planning Committee meetings of 1941 repeatedly emphasised the need to avoid anything in the anti-gossip campaign which might cause spy mania and 'ordinary people to look at each other with suspicion'.[81]

One reason for the 'bad luck' of the silent column campaign, so Kenneth Clark told the Policy Committee, was that it had coincided with the Ministry's assessment of morale at home by its Wartime Social Survey.[82] Since March 1940 the Home Intelligence Unit had been

Fig 13 A second poster in the anti-gossip campaign, 1940, showing the much used slogan 'Keep mum'. INF 3/229.

[74]INF 13/216 [75]INF 1/849 [76]INF 1/846 [77]INF 1/258 [78]INF 1/849
[79]INF 1/249 [80]INF 3/229 [81]INF 1/249 [82]INF 1/849

using Mass Observation to report on the use of gas masks and shelters, pacifist activities, cinema going, shopping habits and other everyday activities of the public. In April the organisation was employed on a regular basis for £100 a week.[83] Its method, as its name implied, was observation on a basis of indirect interviews and overheard conversations. But by May, Waterfield and Mary Adams felt the need for more statistical and less impressionistic surveys. They commissioned their own Wartime Social Survey to investigate the success of various campaigns such as the Ministry of Food's Kitchen Front instructions.[84] Questioning the public was a necessary part of the Survey's work. The press, led by Hugh Cudlipp who had hit on the phrase 'Cooper's Snoopers', taught the public to resent the questioners. Mary Adams justified the work and complained the press was giving her a bad time. She begged for permission to make the Survey public and so dispel suspicion.[85] But the damage was done.

A more open attitude towards the public by the government may well have prevented some rumours and despondency. Reith had commented in February that the public turned to Lord Haw-Haw for want of adequate news at home.[86] In fact the Ministry of Information generally took the line that as much news as possible should reach the people. Before war began, Waterfield's 'earnest hope' had been 'that there may be no need to impose on the press any form of compulsory censorship during the present emergency.' Instead the Ministry wanted to rely on the 'loyal co-operation' of the press who would submit material voluntarily for vetting by the Ministry and take note of the Ministry's Defence Notices forbidding discussion of certain topics.[87] Letters on the same file show that John Beresford tried in vain to get the Services to allow the press more flexibility in describing the numbers and movements of troops. Kenneth Clark considered that the crisis in June 1940 warranted an extension of censorship, but neither he nor Monckton wanted to do more than 'appeal to editors' not to publish articles which might lower morale.[88] In the dark spring of 1942 Ministry officials persuaded the Services and Foreign Office that stricter censorship should be confined only to matters of vital military security.[89] The House of Commons were told firmly in April 1943 that the Ministry would not consider the extension of censorship.[90] Compulsion was always ruled out by officials.

A flexible system of voluntary censorship meant good Ministry relations with the press. Relations with the BBC were also vital to the smooth running of the Ministry. One of Churchill's first instructions to Cooper demanded 'some proposals from you for establishing a more effective control over the BBC'.[91] Cooper later brought in advisers from the Foreign Office and Home Office to act as liaison officers between himself and the BBC and so establish better links. Meanwhile he assured the Prime Minister that all official broadcast announcements

[83]INF 1/262 [84]INF 1/263 [85]INF 1/697 [86]INF 1/867 [87]INF 1/181
[88]INF 1/256 [89]FO 800/277 [90]INF 1/870 [91]INF 1/869

would come through the Ministry. He also told Churchill he intended to 'broadcast himself fairly frequently in order to comment upon and explain the news'. In an earlier draft of this memorandum on the file he strongly recommended other Ministers also to make contact with the public by radio[92] (*fig. 14*). The people wanted and deserved as much factual information as they could safely be given. Hence the insistence,

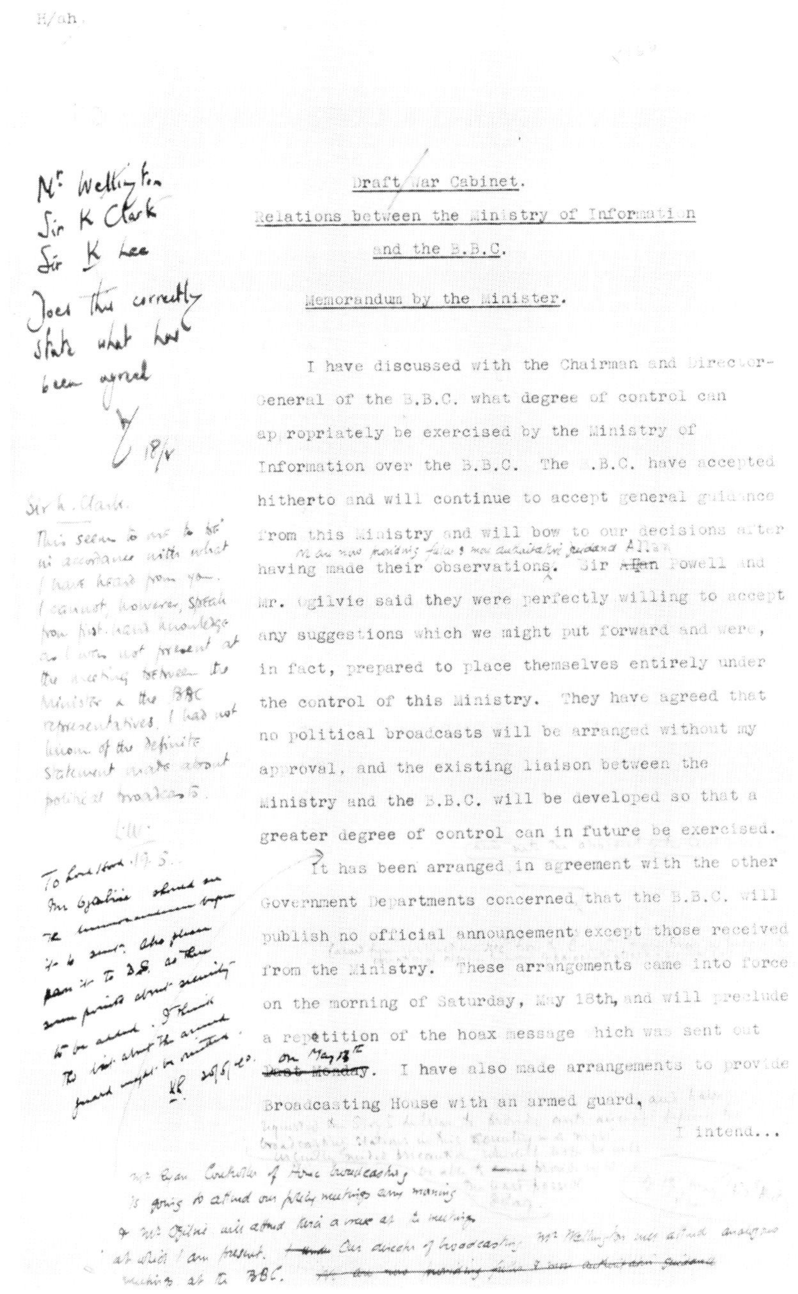

Mr Wellington
Sir K Clark
Sir K Lee

Does this correctly
state what has
been agreed

18/v

Draft War Cabinet.

Relations between the Ministry of Information and the B.B.C.

Memorandum by the Minister.

I have discussed with the Chairman and Director-General of the B.B.C. what degree of control can appropriately be exercised by the Ministry of Information over the B.B.C. The B.B.C. have accepted hitherto and will continue to accept general guidance from this Ministry and will bow to our decisions after having made their observations. Sir Allan Powell and Mr. Ogilvie said they were perfectly willing to accept any suggestions which we might put forward and were, in fact, prepared to place themselves entirely under the control of this Ministry. They have agreed that no political broadcasts will be arranged without my approval, and the existing liaison between the Ministry and the B.B.C. will be developed so that a greater degree of control can in future be exercised.

It has been arranged in agreement with the other Government Departments concerned that the B.B.C. will publish no official announcement except those received from the Ministry. These arrangements came into force on the morning of Saturday, May 18th, and will preclude a repetition of the hoax message which was sent out on May 13th. I have also made arrangements to provide Broadcasting House with an armed guard, and ... I intend...

Fig 14 Conclusion to a memorandum by Duff Cooper just after he had become Minister of Information in May 1940.

DC Duff Cooper
H Viscount Hood, Private Secretary to the Minister
LW Linsay Wellington

INF 1/869

[92] INF 1/869

too, of Ministry officials on the importance of meetings for public discussion.[93] The public must be involved, not frightened: then the rumours would stop. As an official pointed out, 'The keynote of all this is that it is a People's War'.[94] By August 1940 the Planning Committee agreed that 'Exhortation must be as far as possible abandoned. The word 'morale' must not be used again. People must on no account be told to be brave. In future the Ministry would restrict its role to information and explanation'.[95]

[93]INF 1/294 [94]INF 1/527 [95]INF 1/252

4. Blitz August 1940–July 1941: Information

BARTER

German planes bombed British convoys in the Channel in July, Kent fighter bases in August; on 7 September they began the night raids on London and then spread the attack to the Provinces. By July 1941, 43000 civilians had been killed and two and a half million had lost their homes. How did the public cope with the onslaught and how did the Ministry of Information cope with them?

The resolution of August 1940 to eschew all vague exhortation was not immediately honoured. Posters shouted 'Back Them Up' under pictures of fighting spitfires, battleships or commandos; and 'Go to It' over the signature of Herbert Morrison, appointed Home Secretary in October[96] (*fig. 15*). That same month a member of the Planning Committee told Kenneth Clark he had 'voiced a protest against another exhortation' in the form of the Prime Minister's portrait over the slogan 'Keep at It', but had been overruled by his committee.[97] In May 1941 the Ministry's director of press and public relations, Francis Williams, advocated a propaganda campaign 'to reinforce confidence and build a moral defence against the effects of a return of heavy bombing'.[98] While stressing the necessity for more facts and explanation, his 'theme' was mainly the importance of stressing democracy as a way of life. Considering a redraft of the proposed campaign in September, the Home Planning Committee asked 'whether it was really thought necessary to have a specific campaign to improve morale in general'.[99] The blitz had confirmed what most officials had already suspected: that pleas to 'keep at it' or 'Go to It' had less effect on people emerging shocked from shelters to find their homes in rubble than one night without bombs or one victory on the battlefront.

But the Ministry could help morale by telling the public clearly what to do in the emergency. Incendiary bombs and fires were the worst hazard of the raids. The effort to be humorous in illustrating the responsibilities and pitfalls of compulsory fire watching did not disguise a disdain for the public. Incompetent 'half-trained Harry' was not so far from the official view of 'everyman';[100] and the spelling out of simple fire-fighting instructions in great detail was more than a little patronising. More useful, although a little late, were the million and a half leaflets for fire-fighting squads showing the correct use of stirrup pumps and sandbags which the Home Planning Committee reported ready for circulation in January 1941.[101]

---

[96]INF 2/72; INF 13/213 [97]INF 1/249 [98]INF 1/255 [99]INF 1/249 [100]INF 2/73
[101]INF 1/249

A British "Commando" raid on a German-held port in Norway

BACK THEM UP!

Information about shelters was also distributed in leaflet form. In October 1940 the Home Planning Committee approved a proposal for a million copies of a pamphlet giving details of public shelters to be distributed 'to householders in all the chief urban areas subject to attack'.[102] Instructions were also provided for making cheap sleeping bags and 'hay bottles' to keep drinks hot.[103] Posters showed how to make heaters out of flower pots and hot bottles out of bricks heated in the oven for two hours before the raid![104] The public did not like the trench shelters – whose grassy mounds are still visible in some London parks – built for short day-time raids. In London they felt safer in the underground tube stations. In vain did the Ministry organise a special campaign to popularise the surface shelters.[105] Posters, press announcements, broadcasts and newsreels emphasised their superiority over the underground – or any basement – shelters where flooding was always a risk during bombing. But most Londoners during the blitz continued to flock in the early evening to the stations where they at least had space to lie down for the night. Henry Moore's pictures of lines of sleeping bodies on the platforms are a permanent witness to the Ministry's inability to persuade the public out of the underground. Like Paul Nash's elegant aircraft and Stanley Spencer's dockyard scenes they were a product of the War Artists Advisory Committee (WAAC) set up in November. The WAAC commissioned pictures on war themes of their own choice from well-known painters and showed them at regular exhibitions throughout the war[106] (*fig. 16*). Many can now be seen at the Tate Gallery. Exhibitions of weapons, planes and tanks were also organised by the Ministry – often making swift use of bombed sites as in the case of the John Lewis store in Oxford Street, blitzed on 27 September 1940.

Eventually the Ministry accepted the public choice of the tubes as their shelters. The Home Planning Committee then devised a code of shelter behaviour advocating cleanliness and discipline, mutual toleration and friendliness – and the use of ear plugs to aid sleep.[107] Leaflets with this advice probably had as little effect on life in the shelters as the 'Mightier Yet' posters left over from the earlier campaign and stuck up on the curving tube walls. Another leaflet was designed to help the public when they emerged from the shelters. 'After the Raid' told them to go to rest centres – with directions from ARP wardens or the police – if they had nowhere to sleep and eat; that they would be given travel vouchers to join relatives, compensation for damaged property, injury allowances if they had lost limbs and pensions if they had lost the family wage earner.[108] After a member of the committee complained that the first draft of the text was 'more informative than reassuring' the last sentence was changed: the public was assured that 'The Government' as well as 'your fellow citizens and your neighbours' see 'that "front line" fighters are looked after'.

But the Ministry was beginning to accept that its task was in fact to

---

[102]INF 1/251 [103]INF 1/252 [104]INF 13/151 [105]INF 1/249 [106]INF 13/213
[107]INF 1/249 [108]INF 1/339

Fig 15 A poster in the 'Back them up' series, 1940. INF 2/72.

Convoy   *Norman Wilkinson, O.B.E., P.R.I.*

War Pictures
BY BRITISH ARTISTS

NATIONAL GALLERY
Trafalgar Square

WEEKDAYS 10 A.M. TO 5 P.M. SUNDAYS 2 P.M. TO 5 P.M.

ADMISSION FREE

provide information rather than either exhortation or reassurance. Asked by the War Cabinet Committee in February 1941 to produce yet another leaflet – this time on the continuing possibility of invasion – officials agreed to do so. Their Home Intelligence reports told them that 53 per cent of the population not only expected an invasion but thought the Germans would soon be 'cut to pieces'. They were asking for more guidance about the duties of civilians when the enemy landed. Churchill was asked to produce an introductory message to the leaflet. It was suggested this should be specific in its order to 'stay put'. The Prime Minister's preference for the phrase 'stand firm' with its over-tones of general exhortation was not welcomed by the officials. They concentrated on the practical problems envisaged after invasion: the distribution of news, the prevention of bogus broadcasting and the adequate identification of official loudspeaker vans.[109] The text was eventually agreed and the leaflet produced[110] (*fig. 17*). It was stored for the emergency by the GPO in spite of the latter's refusal to guarantee that the pamphlets on the dangers of gas already in its vaults would not be sent out by mistake. By the autumn the threat had disappeared. The film division objected to the suggestion they should make another film about a future invasion. And the new Director General, Cyril Radcliffe, told Findlater Stewart, now at the Home Defence Executive, that 'invasion propaganda would fall dead on the public at present' and even be regarded as a government stunt to divert attention from the bad news in North Africa, Greece and Crete.

Conscious efforts at morale raising were not entirely abandoned during the bombing. The idea of using special numbers of periodicals for propaganda had been accepted earlier when a *Picture Post* issue on 'The Might of Britain' had been planned as part of the reassurance campaign. Extra pages were to be financed by the MOI with a special Treasury grant but the idea was dropped for financial reasons.[111] In August 1940, an issue did appear on air raids, and in September the part played by the RAF in the Battle of Britain was featured in *Illustrated*. Five-minute shorts were commissioned by the film division: telephone girls carried on working near unexploded bombs; and men stayed late at the factory, knowing the best way to protect their families was to turn out more weapons.[112] Humphrey Jennings's documentary for the Ministry on the blitz, 'London can Take It', was a more subtle exercise on the same theme. Films on shelter life, 'Adjustment to the Blitz' and on 'Osterley Park' – about Home Guard training – were instructive and indirectly morale raising.[113] The publicity division handed out stories of 'our phlegmatic islanders in the blitz' to the press, encouraging cartoons like the picture of the housewife clearing up the dust that had come through her broken window saying 'Well, there's one thing about this Blitz, it keeps you busy and you forget the war'. But the Ministry clamped down on specific stories of heroism. This was not only because they considered such propaganda ineffective but because such reports might be useful to the enemy. Mary Adams wrote a furious note to

Fig 16   Poster advertising an exhibition sponsored by the War Artists Advisory Committee. INF 13/213 part 2.

Fig 17   Leaflet issued in spring 1941 INF 13/219/2. (*See overleaf*).

[109]INF 1/880 [110]INF 13/219 [111]INF 1/234 [112]INF 1/209 [113]INF 1/251

IMPORTANT NOTICE INF 13/210/2

This leaflet is being distributed throughout the country. If invasion comes it applies in this town as elsewhere, but before invasion comes those who are not engaged on useful work should leave this town—see special posters and leaflets.

Issued by the Ministry of Information *in co-operation with the War Office and the Ministry of Home Security*

Beating the INVADER

A MESSAGE FROM THE PRIME MINISTER

IF invasion comes, everyone—young or old, men and women—will be eager to play their part worthily. By far the greater part of the country will not be immediately involved. Even along our coasts, the greater part will remain unaffected. But where the enemy lands, or tries to land, there will be most violent fighting. Not only will there be the battles when the enemy tries to come ashore, but afterwards there will fall upon his lodgments very heavy British counter-attacks, and all the time the lodgments will be under the heaviest attack by British bombers. The fewer civilians or non-combatants in these areas, the better—apart from essential workers who must remain. So if you are advised by the authorities to leave the place where you live, it is your duty to go elsewhere when you are told to leave. When the attack begins, it will be too late to go; and, unless you receive definite instructions to move, your duty then will be to stay where you are. You will have to get into the safest place you can find, and stay there until the battle is over. For all of you then the order and the duty will be: " STAND FIRM ".

This also applies to people inland if any considerable number of parachutists or air-borne troops are landed in their neighbourhood. Above all, they must not cumber the roads. Like their fellow-countrymen on the coasts, they must " STAND FIRM ". The Home Guard, supported by strong mobile columns wherever the enemy's numbers require it, will immediately come to grips with the invaders, and there is little doubt will soon destroy them.

Throughout the rest of the country where there is no fighting going on and no close cannon fire or rifle fire can be heard, everyone will govern his conduct by the second great order and duty, namely, " CARRY ON ". It may easily be some weeks before the invader has been totally destroyed, that is to say, killed or captured to the last man who has landed on our shores. Meanwhile, all work must be continued to the utmost, and no time lost.

The following notes have been prepared to tell everyone in rather more detail what to do, and they should be carefully studied. Each man and woman should think out a clear plan of personal action in accordance with the general scheme

Winston S. Churchill

STAND FIRM

I. What do I do if fighting breaks out in my neighbourhood?

Keep indoors or in your shelter until the battle is over. If you can have a trench ready in your garden or field, so much the better. You may want to use it for protection if your house is damaged. But if you are at work, or if you have special orders, carry on as long as possible and only take cover when danger approaches. If you are on your way to work, finish your journey if you can.

If you see an enemy tank, or a few enemy soldiers, do not assume that the enemy are in control of the area. What you have seen may be a party sent on in advance, or stragglers from the main body who can easily be rounded up

CARRY ON

2. What do I do in areas which are some way from the fighting?

Stay in your district and carry on. Go to work whether in shop, field, factory or office. Do your shopping, send your children to school until you are told not to. Do not try to go and live somewhere else. Do not use the roads for any unnecessary journey; they must be left free for troop movements even a long way from the district where actual fighting is taking place.

3. Will certain roads and railways be reserved for the use of the Military, even in areas far from the scene of action?

Yes, certain roads will have to be reserved for important troop movements; but such reservations should be only temporary. As far as possible, bus companies and railways will try to maintain essential public services, though it may be necessary to cut these down. Bicyclists and pedestrians may use the roads for journeys to work, unless instructed not to do so.

ADVICE AND ORDERS

4. Whom shall I ask for advice?

The police and A.R.P. wardens.

5. From whom shall I take orders?

In most cases from the police and A.R.P. wardens. But there may be times when you will have to take orders from the military and the Home Guard in uniform.

6. Is there any means by which I can tell that an order is a true order and not faked?

You will generally know your policeman and your A.R.P. wardens by sight, and can trust them. With a bit of common sense you can tell if a soldier is really British or only pretending to be so. If in doubt ask a policeman, or ask a soldier whom you know personally.

INSTRUCTIONS

7. What does it mean when the church bells are rung?

It is a warning to the local garrison that troops have been seen landing from the air in the neighbourhood of the church in question. Church bells will *not* be rung all over the country as a general warning that invasion has taken place. The ringing of church bells in one place will not be taken up in neighbouring churches.

8. Will instructions be given over the wireless?

Yes; so far as possible. But remember that the enemy can overhear any wireless message, so that the wireless cannot be used for instructions which might give him valuable information.

9. In what other ways will instructions be given?

Through the Press; by loudspeaker vans; and perhaps by leaflets and posters. But remember that genuine Government leaflets will be given to you only by the policeman, your A.R.P. warden or your postman; while genuine posters and instructions will be put up only on Ministry of Information notice boards and official sites, such as police stations, post offices, A.R.P. posts, town halls and schools.

FOOD

10. Should I try to lay in extra food?

No. If you have already laid in a stock of food, keep it for a real emergency; but do not add to it. The Government has made arrangements for food supplies.

NEWS

11. Will normal news services continue?

Yes. Careful plans have been made to enable newspapers and wireless broadcasts to carry on, and in case of need there are emergency measures which will bring you the news. But if there should be some temporary breakdown in news supply, it is very important that you should not listen to rumours nor pass them on, but should wait till real news comes through again. Do not use the telephones or send telegrams if you can possibly avoid it.

MOTOR-CARS

12. Should I put my car, lorry or motor-bicycle out of action?

Yes, when you are told to do so by the police, A.R.P. wardens or military; or when it is obvious that there is an immediate risk of its being seized by the enemy—then disable and hide your bicycle and destroy your maps.

13. How should it be put out of action?

Remove distributor head and leads and either empty the tank or remove the carburettor. If you don't know how to do this, find out now from your nearest garage. In the case of diesel engines remove the injection pump and connection. The parts removed must be hidden well away from the vehicle.

THE ENEMY

14. Should I defend myself against the enemy?

The enemy is not likely to turn aside to attack separate houses. If small parties are going about threatening persons and property in an area not under enemy control and come your way, you have the right of every man and woman to do what you can to protect yourself, your family and your home.

GIVE ALL THE HELP YOU CAN TO OUR TROOPS

Do not tell the enemy anything

Do not give him anything

Do not help him in any way

(1649) 59978 Wt. 46531/P1009 250M 5/41 W.P. Ltd. Gp. 8

35

Macadam complaining that a broadcast emphasised the 'usual smiles' and 'sense of pride' of the people of Swansea after they had been bombed. And a Coventry woman wrote to the Ministry making the same point: 'We have enough clearing up to do without your people inviting another blitz. Tell them we are blotted out and let us get on with the job'.[114] It was also vital, Nicolson reminded his Minister in a memorandum, to prevent the press publishing news to the effect that factories in any given area had resumed working.[115]

In any case, such broadcasts seemed to be unnecessary. Naturally, there were instances of low morale: the weekly reports drawn up by the Home Intelligence Division on the basis of information from regional officers do not give an undiluted picture of heroism and courage during the raids. Morale in Birmingham was particularly bad after its night of bombing late in November 1940.[116] Criticism of the civic organisation was reported from Plymouth where power was said to be concentrated 'in a few elderly hands'.[117] Physical fatigue was taking its toll by May 1941.[118] Even with hindsight the regional officers in their histories of their local offices requested by the Ministry in 1945 – and incidentally providing a superb historical source – stressed the misery as well as the bravery of the public. The account of the people of Portsmouth 'trekking' every night to sleep in the surrounding countryside to avoid the bombs is particularly poignant.[119] Nevertheless, the reports describe 'the extraordinary resilience' shown by the people under bombardment. The Home Intelligence report of 14 October 1940 commented that raids seemed to be accepted as part of an unpleasant routine. Officials seemed surprised at the considerate behaviour reported in the shelters[120] and also by the letters from factory managers commending the calmness of their employees. Their faith in the public was not yet strong: they were more affected by one report of panic in the East End of London than by many stories of high morale.[121] The decision to cut down on general exhortation was due as much to a feeling of impotence as to any belief that the people could 'take it'.

The Ministry was not always willing to take the public into its confidence. Demands for reprisals after the raid on Coventry in November 1940 and on Plymouth in March 1941 were included in regional reports.[122] Local officers were instructed to prevent discontent against the government by using the expediency argument: 'From the point of view of winning the war it pays to use what resources we have to bomb military objectives'.[123] The film division came up with a script, 'A Target is Bombed' to emphasise the carefully planned destruction of arms factories as opposed to indiscriminate bombing of towns.[124] Betjeman was told the project justified an expenditure of £3,000. The film became the very successful 'Target for Tonight'. By 1942, when German civilians were indeed bombed, the Ministry did its best to keep the new policy from the people. Its reason could have been guilt; or it could have been the wish to keep from the public their belief that the

---

[114]INF 1/174 [115]INF 1/845 [116]INF 1/845 [117]INF 1/292 [118]INF 1/292
[119]INF 1/297 [120]INF 1/294 [121]INF 1/64 [122]INF 1/292 [123]INF 1/672 [124]INF 1/210

war might be won or lost through the vulnerability of a people's morale – German or British.

Duff Cooper did want the public to have details of home raids and casualties. Lack of information, officials had already learnt, meant a less willing participation in the war effort. A fierce argument was waged with the Air Ministry over the publication of the names of bombed towns, especially after the failure to report the Birmingham raid had angered its citizens. They didn't care how much they were knocked about, reported their MP, but they wanted their fellow countrymen to know about it. The people of Bristol, too, were furious that their raid received less publicity than Coventry's blitz. Cyril Radcliffe, as yet Deputy Director General, drew up a draft letter to Morrison for Duff Cooper to sign asking him to countermand the Air Ministry's ruling that bombed towns could not be named by the press: the Germans obviously already knew what towns they were bombing and 'there are, believe me, more important considerations at stake . . . It seems to me plain that we cannot go on in this way if the public are to retain any respect at all for the official attitude towards news'.[125]

In fact, as Radcliffe's draft implied, the Ministry was still feeling insecure in face of pressure from the Service ministries. Director General Monckton in May 1941 wrote a long and bitter joint memorandum with Radcliffe to Cooper, claiming that while the raw material of propaganda was news and information, the MOI had no control over either: 'It can decide neither *what* to make public nor *when* to make something public nor what line or shape to give to such information as is made public'.[126] The refusal to allow the Ministry to make propaganda out of the arrival of Hess – by emphasising a split amongst the German leaders – tipped Monckton's frustration towards resignation.[127] His minister, in a long hand-written diatribe against 'the misbegotten freak bred from the unnatural union between Sir Horace Wilson and Sir Samuel Hoare', nevertheless pointed out that the Ministry's position had improved since its increased control over the BBC, while its relations with the press were on the mend. Monckton reluctantly agreed to stay; he took his minister's advice to revise his memorandum for the Prime Minister. The War Cabinet decided that the Ministry of Information should be the central agency for the conduct of all government publicity; all propaganda on behalf of any Department had in future to be conducted through the MOI. But departmental ministers were to 'retain their right to veto, or require the publication of, particular facts or statements where they think it necessary to do so in the interests of national security'.[128] The battle with the Air Ministry was lost; the single control of the issuing of news demanded by Monckton for the MOI was never won. Eventually, in July 1941, it was Cooper who first asked Churchill to release him. Monckton followed suit in December.

[125]INF 1/846 [126]INF 1/857 [127]INF 1/912 [128]CAB 66/17.WP (41) 149

5. Allies and Enemies 1941-5: The Limits of Persuasion

NO FURTHER
TERRITORIAL AMBITION

Brendan Bracken succeeded Duff Cooper. Lack of ministerial experience did not prevent him giving the MOI a new cohesion even in the black eighteen months before Stalingrad and El Alamein. His childhood in Ireland and Australia had given him sympathy with people struggling for survival; his successful ventures in the London newspaper world had taught him how to get on with the press. Most important of all, he was not only a close friend of the Prime Minister but a friend to whom Churchill listened. His objection to an enquiry by a sub-committee of the War Cabinet into censorship was accepted by the Prime Minister with an uncharacteristic apology. Churchill told the Secretary to the Cabinet 'to remove the passage from the records'; and Bracken to 'please leave off scolding me on paper and if you have any griefs come and beat me up personally'.[120] When he was forced by Churchill to suppress 'this foolish production' of the film 'Colonel Blimp' making good-humoured fun of the army leadership, Bracken was not too shy to point out that the censorship had merely given the film 'a wonderful advertisement'.[130]

Bracken had a good relationship, too, with Walter Monckton and Cyril Radcliffe. All were in harmony when it came to discussing Bracken's first main problem on taking office: how should Britain's new ally be presented to the public? Russia had been attacked by Hitler in June 1941 and was now fighting Britain's war with her. But the government, not least the Ministry of Information, had been fearful since the war began that disaffection among the people would lead to a communist rising. Hence their close watch on pacifist and communist publications and their failure to object too strongly to the Home Office's decision to shut down the *Daily Worker* even though they argued against stricter censorship. Reports of high sales of the communist paper in the shelters had worried officials; but they had never advocated a strong line against the Party. The fact that Russia was now a friend meant an additional boost for the British Communist Party. A long memorandum by the Director of the Home Division warned that 'the political theory of Communism has now both an audience and an occasion and that it is necessary to counterpose it'.[131] Direct anti-communist propaganda would only exacerbate the situation. But by stressing 'continually our longing for individual liberty and freedom of choice' a campaign might subtly persuade the public of the evils of Bolshevism. Monckton passed on the advice to Bracken[132] (*fig. 18*).

[129]INF 1/859 [130]PREM 4/14/15 [131]INF 1/913 [132]INF 1/913

Major Morton's minute to P.M. returned to No.10 8/9/41

1. Mr Parker
2. D.G.
3. Parl. Sec.

The Minister would be glad to receive your recommendations upon the attached minute.

BCS
3/9

To: The Minister.
From: D.G.

I do not think that we ought to hesitate to emphasise in our propaganda the divergence between our own political conception and Communism any more than we ought to let the Communist Party in this country take credit for the help which the Russian defence is giving us. The Communist Party of Great Britain did not support our war; they only support our war effort now because we are fighting the same enemy as the Soviet in whose war they do believe.

But I think it would be a mistake to make our main-effort criticism destructive of the Soviet ideology. It would be better to throw up in positive contrast the enduring value of our own democratic way of political life.

Subject to your direction I should propose to give instructions on these lines. Indeed, I did so at the Policy Committee Meeting this morning.

W.M.
4.9.41

I agree with the guidelines embodied in this minute.   E.T. 5/9.

Churchill accepted the idea of a strong propaganda campaign in praise of the new ally with absolutely no mention of communism. An Anglo-Soviet liaison section was set up in the Ministry in August. Its head announced that publicity for Russia would 'steal the thunder' of the British communists and sabotage their efforts.[133] Thus behind the 'Tanks for Russia' week in the factories, the poster illustrating Anglo-Russian co-operation, together with the photographic exhibitions celebrating Russia's economic progress lay the Ministry's fear of communism at home[134] (fig. 3). It was responsible, too, for the elaborate celebration organised by the publicity division, of Red Army Day on 21 February 1943 to commemorate the Russian victories. In the Albert Hall the military strength of the ally was saluted – and the salute preserved in a series of photographs;[135] her five year plan was praised in a play hastily written by the poet Louis Macneice.[136]

Fig 18   Memorandum from Walter Monckton as Director General of the Ministry of Information to Brendan Bracken as Minister, on problems of handling pro-Soviet propaganda.
WM Walter Monckton
ET   Ernest Thurtle, Parliamentary Secretary
INF 1/913.

[133]INF 1/147 [134]INF 1/249 [135]INF 2/42 [136]FO 371/36973

Fig 19   Leaflet welcoming US servicemen
to Britain, 1942. INF 2/1.

Arrangements for this will be made by the Naval authorities at the port at which your ship is lying. Your Captain will tell you when you are required.

WATCH THE TRAFFIC!

WE drive on the left of the road. You drive on the right. You may think this won't affect you unless you drive a car, but it does. When you cross a road, for example, you've got to look *right* and then *left*. When you call a taxi try to do it from the *left* side of the road and don't try to get in the cab from the right-hand side.

CAMERAS

CAMERAS may seem to you innocent things, but they are not to us. In the interests of security, cameras may not be carried in certain places, and these are almost certain to include the port at which you arrive. Since the beginning of the war it is forbidden to take photographs of lots of places and things, so you had better ask the advice of the police before you try to use your camera. In fact, if you take our advice you won't try to take a camera ashore at all, but will content yourself with buying photographs.

CANTEENS

YOU will find Navy, Army and Air Force Canteens in nearly

6

all the ports of the United Kingdom. They are known as N.A.A.F.I. for short. Provided you have appropriate identity papers, these canteens are open to you, as are all Service Canteens operated by voluntary societies in ports and railway stations.

Some of these canteens are small and sometimes over-crowded. There may be a shortage of cigarettes in these canteens (in other words — maybe if you're lucky you'll be able to buy cigarettes). Don't blame the help, who are frequently voluntary workers and doing their best.

FOOD AND CLOTHING RESTRICTIONS

FOOD is adequate for all reasonable people, although pressure on shipping space has made it necessary to cut down individual supplies. Rationing has been introduced for meat, bacon, eggs, butter, margarine, cooking fats, cheese, sugar, jam, milk, tea, onions, canned fruit (the consumption of oranges is practically limited to children), and most dried and canned food — to put everybody on the same level. It is not, at present, necessary for you to have food coupons to get meals in restaurants. Recently clothing has also been rationed, but merchant seamen may obtain coupons from Mercantile Marine Offices. (*See* page 11.) Any number of people, official and unofficial, will be eager to tell you how to go about this rationing business, but unless you are ashore more than five days it need not concern you.

7

CURRENCY

ONE of our quaint English customs is to make the currency as difficult as possible for everybody, including ourselves. You can take it roughly that five shillings (better known as five bob) are equivalent to a dollar. Watch the half crown and the two shilling piece – they're very similar in size and design, but the half crown is worth 10 cents more. Various wartime measures have been introduced in this country relating to foreign currency, so please don't try to exchange money except through your own officials or a British bank. Here's a rough guide to the values.

Coin	Slang Name	Metal	Value
Half penny	Copper	copper	1 cent
Penny		copper	2 cents
Three pence (Threepenny bit)		silver or twelve-cornered brass	5 cents
Sixpence	Tanner	silver	10 cents
Shilling	Bob	silver	20 cents
Two shilling piece (Florin)		silver	40 cents
Half crown	Half-dollar	silver	50 cents
Ten shillings	Ten bob	paper (purple)	2 dollars
Pound	Quid	paper (blue & brown)	4 dollars

THE enemy has a weakness for printing British paper money which we don't want to encourage, so we don't let any bills in except through certain official channels. It is important therefore for you to remember to get rid of paper money *before* you leave the country. This does not necessarily mean that you must spend it. We suggest you hand back to the Captain of your ship *before* you sail any unspent money and ask him to credit you with the value in U.S. currency. Actually it is forbidden to take British currency out of the country.

8

HALF PENNY

SIXPENCE

ONE PENNY

SHILLING

PENNY

THREE PENCE (Silver)

TWO SHILLING PIECE

THREE PENCE (Brass)

HALF CROWN

9

MAIL RATES TO U.S.A.

AIR MAIL	½ oz.	1s. 3d.
	(and 1s. 3d. for each subsequent half-ounce).	
SURFACE MAIL	1 oz.	2½d.
	(and 1d. for each subsequent ounce).	

INFORMATION TO THE ENEMY

ONE of the enemy's chief sources of information is the soldier or sailor himself. A few odd words to a casual acquaintance in a bar (or in a café or a church or a bus) may fill the blank in an enemy report. The man who talks about his unit in public is risking his friends' lives and his own. Leakage of information is a serious problem. Keep quiet about yourself and about your unit or ship.

AMERICAN CONSULATES

YOUR first contact will doubtless be with your own Consul, and, of course, he will give you all the help he can. Here is a list of addresses in the principal towns.

TOWN	ADDRESS	TELEPHONE NO.
BELFAST	1, Donegall Square South	BELFAST 21858
BIRMINGHAM	Neville House, Waterloo Street	MIDLAND 2582
BRISTOL	18, Baldwin Street	BRISTOL 25027
BRADFORD	Britannia House, Leeds Road	BRADFORD 1275
CARDIFF	Royal Chambers, Park Place	CARDIFF 4081

10

TOWN	ADDRESS	TELEPHONE NO.
EDINBURGH	71, George Street	EDINBURGH 24606
GLASGOW	55, West Regent Street	DOUGLAS 3216
LIVERPOOL	Cunard Buildings, Pier Head	CITY 66
LONDON	1, Grosvenor Square, S.W.1	GROSVENOR 4111
MANCHESTER	Arkwright House, Parsonage Gardens	DEANSGATE 4187
NEWCASTLE-ON-TYNE	The Newe House, 10 & 12, Pilgrim Street	NEWCASTLE 23591
PLYMOUTH	1, The Crescent	PLYMOUTH 5663

The following is of special interest to American Merchant Seamen:

SUPERINTENDENTS OF MERCANTILE MARINE OFFICES

AMERICAN merchant seamen will find that the Superintendents of the Mercantile Marine Offices will be a ready source of information on all matters concerning them and about which it is not necessary to trouble their Consul. There are offices at all ports and their addresses are well known to people in the dock area.

TOWN	ADDRESS	TELEPHONE NO.
CARDIFF	Bute Docks	CARDIFF 8980
GLASGOW	4-12, James Watt Street	CENTRAL 7166
LIVERPOOL	Cornhill, Liverpool 1	ROYAL 4747
LONDON	Dock Street, London, E.1	ROYAL 1978-9
NEWCASTLE-ON-TYNE	Westgate Road	NEWCASTLE 22216
BELFAST	Custom House	BELFAST 22678
BRISTOL	Old Library, King Street	BRISTOL 22933
LEITH	Custom House, Leith, Edinburgh	LEITH 35809

11

By the time of Red Army Day the public were more excited by the victories of their other allies, the Americans, in North Africa. The Ministry had for some time used the media to try to improve Anglo-American relations. In July 1940 a special issue of *Picture Post* – circulated both at home and in the United States – emphasised the historic and cultural links between the countries in an attempt to counter American isolationism. R.A. Bevan, under pressure from the American divisions of the Ministry, used his influence with the Ministry of Supply to get sufficient paper for the issue.[137] After Pearl Harbour eventually brought the Americans into the war, the problem of the Ministry was how to preserve good relations between American troops and British civilians. A pamphlet was issued to the GIs welcoming them to the country and explaining aspects of British life – and incidentally providing a useful guide to the coinage, rationing system and attitudes of 1942[138] (*fig. 19*). Regional officers described how it became necessary during 1943 to billet some of the US troops on householders and how the operation had actually improved relations.[139] By 1944 one and a half million American troops were stationed in the country. A Home Intelligence special report on the attitude of younger people to them did not come up with the expected story of resentment. Complaints of cockiness, boastfulness, drunkenness and their much envied high pay were balanced by reports of friendly hospitality.[140] Bracken reported to the War Cabinet that 'reports on the British reaction to their visitors are genuinely favourable'.[141] He also told his colleagues he would not initiate any campaign to deal with the problem of the coloured troops: 'I do not think that the mass of the civilian population ought to be approached at all with any propaganda on the subject. A strong step would be disastrous and there is not sufficient prospect of any real success, however wise one's attitude'.[142] Bracken understood the limits of influence of his Ministry: it could not attempt to change basic attitudes. Nor could it expect to be very effective in making the public more aware of Japan as the enemy. Posters went up announcing in Churchill's words that the war against Japan would be fought to the very end. But Bracken pointed out to the Cabinet in June 1943 that the Ministry could not overcome the public feeling that this enemy was a relatively distant threat.[143]

It was of course much easier to rouse public emotion against the Germans, 26 miles from British shores and too often overhead. Exaggerating the dangers of defeatism during the summer of 1940, officials wasted time devising an 'anger campaign' to whip up feeling against the enemy.[144] Their patronising adjectives showed how little they identified with the public: 'The ordinary people in the little homes on which fall the day to day strains of this war' had to be incensed against Germany by posters, pamphlets, films and broadcasts. Policy Committee minutes of January 1941 show the Ministry were still concerned to counteract the attitude 'that a German victory would not

[137]INF 1/234 [138]INF 2/1/2105 [139]INF 1/297 [140]INF 1/293 [141]CAB 66/28. WP (42) 385
[142]CAB 66/29. WP (42) 459 [143]CAB 66/37. WP (43) 238 [144]INF 1/251

Children into Ruffians

THE NEW NAZI EDUCATION

make very much difference'. The public must be convinced of the increasing brutality of the Germans, especially since 'the departure of eminent men of science and culture'. Kenneth Clark thought 'the line we should take in home propaganda was that the enemy were much worse and that we should emphasise wherever possible the wickedness and evil perpetrated in the occupied countries'.[145] The Home Planning Committee produced a memorandum fully justifying any publicity of the 'evil things which confront us' in order 'to fortify the will to continue the struggle'.[146] This was the thinking behind the pamphlets on Nazi education[147] (*fig. 20*); on 'German industry through peace and war' pointing out that 'industrial power without conscience can

---

[145]INF 1/849 [146]INF 1/251 [147]INF 2/1

Fig 20 Leaflet expounding some of the horrors of Nazism, 1941. INF 2/1. (*Continued overleaf*)

Once the individual had value, but now . . .

The aim of education, as understood by civilised peoples, is to bring out the best in each individual. For it is the free play of intellect and personality that gives life both meaning and savour, and renders possible a worth-while existence for every citizen.

But in Germany to-day all this is changed. Men and women belong not to themselves but to the State; and the State belongs to tyrants. To keep their subjects down, these tyrants must do more than suppress liberty of opinion and access to knowledge in the adult; they must prevent the minds of children from ever opening, and turn the rising generation into a dull mass of unthinking, regimented and perverted slaves.

Such a mass, mentally stunted and ignorant of the outer world, can be easily imbued with appalling hatred and fanaticism. That is the purpose of its creation; it is avowedly intended as a means to universal conquest, from the threat of which no corner of the globe is safe.

2

Each child is but a unit in the national stock-farm

" We start with the child when he is three years old. As soon as he begins to think, he gets a little flag put in his hand; then follow the school, the Hitler Youth, the S.A. and military training. We do not let him go; when adolescence is past the Arbeitsfront takes him up again and does not release him till he dies, *whether he likes it or not.*"

Thus Dr. Ley, Nazi Minister of Labour. Hitler had already written in *Mein Kampf* that " the development of mental capacity is of secondary importance "—a statement which Dr. Goebbels improved further by pronouncing, in a short story called *Michael* (1934) : " The intellect is a danger to the shaping of character. We are not on earth to cram our skulls with knowledge. . . . Bring up tough guys! That is what the business of the High School should be."

As for girls, " the one absolute aim of female education must be towards future motherhood" (*Mein Kampf*). There is to be nothing soft or gentle about the Nazi woman; and German girls, no less than their brothers, must subordinate everything to the false obsession of the " Nordic " race.

3

become a Frankenstein'[148]; on 'Europe after Four Years of German Domination'[149]; and on 'Four Under Hitler' describing the tribulations of a French housewife, a Dutch farmer, a Belgian businessman and a Norwegian schoolteacher.[150] Notes for speakers were drawn up telling the public that 'the Nazis stamp out beauty, friendliness, kindness, justice and freedom'.[151] More specific facts were provided on Nazi youth, the destruction of churches in occupied countries and the Gestapo.

Little attention was paid to the concentration camps even though by the winter of 1942-43 some news was filtering through of Hitler's plans for wholesale extermination of the Jews in Poland. This news coincided with a temporary increase in the reports of anti-semitic feeling at home. Although the Ministry's weekly home intelligence reports recorded strong feelings of indignation and horror at the news from the continent, no increase in sympathy with British Jews was apparent. Jews were being accused of profiting from the black market and avoiding conscription. Some members of the Jewish community even feared that too much emphasis on the horrors of the concentration camps might increase anti-semitism at home by drawing attention to Jews, and there was some evidence that this might be so. Not altogether surprisingly,

[148]INF 2/6/144   [149]INF 2/7/156   [150]INF 2/8   [151]INF 1/332

No time for home life, because . . .

The Nazis attained power by a false appeal. The two things most dear to German hearts, they said, were in danger—religion and family life. Both of these a Nazi Government would save.

Yet home life, like traditional religion, scarcely exists now in Nazi Germany. Father must be constantly attending Party meetings, and Mother going to the National Socialist Women's Union. Let either of them show any laxity in this respect, and the dreaded Gestapo will be after them. Disappearance into a concentration camp may follow.

Meanwhile, the sons must give up practically all their spare time to *Hitler Youth* activities, and the daughters their leisure to the *League of German Girls*. It is rarely indeed that all members of the family can be at home together.

The older generation, who remember a saner atmosphere, may resent this bitterly, but the young people are conditioned to it, and willingly accept it. Family ties are kindly and sentimental, whereas the youthful Nazi glories in being hard and unemotional—an automaton among his fellow automata.

Home life would breed the kindly virtues

The Nazi conception has no use either for kindliness or for individual tastes and interests. It is because home life and religion alike foster spiritual independence that home life and religion are both opposed by the Nazis. The home, moreover, is a self-governing unit, a little world of its own—and as such it may be dangerous to Dictators. In the safe privacy of home, people might even begin to think and talk freely!

Unless they join the *Hitler Youth*—" at the end of the school terms the children will be left exclusively to their parents' educational influence, which constitutes the grave danger that the children may be lost to the State. A father who keeps his children away from the *Hitler Youth* abuses his parental power. It will therefore be taken away from him."

This was part of a judgment given by a Children's Court in Saxony, on a father who had dared to try to keep his children at home. It represents a practical application of the doctrine enunciated by Dr. Ley at the Berlin Sports Palace in February, 1937 : "The education of Youth belongs to the *Hitler Youth* alone. We believe in Adolf Hitler alone."

4   5

some people found the stories of concentration camp atrocities 'too horrible even for the Nazis'. Even the partial reports that did reach Britain therefore, were difficult for people to believe. The subject remained a difficult one to handle, by comparison with other tales of Nazi atrocities, and the Ministry steered clear of it throughout the war.[152]

'Atrocity' literature was produced by the Ministry until late in 1944. Like the early anger campaign it was a sign of lack of confidence in the people's natural antipathy to Nazism. Like the silent column campaign it produced its own backlash. Bombarded with pamphlets and encouraged to attend exhibitions on Nazi atrocities, it was difficult for the public to accept the Roosevelt/Churchill promise in their Atlantic Charter in August 1941 of peace and prosperity for all, including the vanquished. The Home Intelligence department was well aware of the problem.

A minute from the Policy to the Publications division quoted Waterfield's warning that it was not 'our public aim to ostracise Germany in perpetuity . . . it cannot be good propaganda to enlarge upon the theme that Germans are a race which has no future in civilisation'.[153] The Director of the division was similarly worried by

[152]INF 1/292; INF 1/251 [153]INF 1/672

the effect of the atrocity literature on public fears 'that the Government would not treat our enemies sufficiently sternly when they had been beaten' – a fear encouraged by Montgomery's entertainment of the German generals after El Alamein.[154]

Once again the policy of exhortation had aroused emotions unhelpful to the overall war effort. But the anti-German propaganda was not a complete fiasco. The 'V for Victory' campaign was originally formulated for occupied countries but then adopted at home. According to the Home Intelligence report at the end of July, it 'had captured the imagination of a large section of the public. Its extensive use in this country by shopkeepers, publicans and writers on walls and public utility vehicles is widely commented on'.[155] One Regional Information Officer (RIO) reported that the public considered the 'V' sign a 'welcome symbol or focal point on which to concentrate their desire for the crushing of Nazism'.[156] Its success was probably related to the fact that the idea appeared to be spontaneous and had – unlike the anti-rumour campaigns – 'no connection in the public mind' with the Ministry.[157]

---

[154]INF 1/284 [155]INF 1/292 [156]INF 1/672 [157]INF 1/292

6. Austerity 1941-5: Instruction

Bracken himself, always unwilling to distinguish between good and bad Germans, supported the atrocity propaganda. But he knew that making the public hate the Germans – or love the Russians while still distrusting Communism – was peripheral to the main task of his Ministry: to explain and instruct. Efforts to influence public emotional attitudes betrayed a lack of confidence. Experience of the blitz had given the officials more faith. Their new minister encouraged it. In October 1941 Stephen Taylor wrote a long annex to the weekly report of his Home Intelligence Division. The document was a patronising, headmasterly report on the morale and behaviour of the public: taste low but common sense high. Most significantly, 'will listen to explanations when it will not accept exhortations'.[158]

In February 1942 Home Intelligence reported 'shock, bewilderment and anger' after German warships had sailed unharmed through the Channel and 'silence too deep for words' after the fall of Singapore.[159] R.H. Parker insisted that 'moral oratory' would be the wrong way to deal with this despondency: 'If the country is given the evidence upon which it can come to a judgment it will judge fairly. That is the summation of nearly three years study of the reactions of public opinion'.[160] This was exactly Brendan Bracken's view. He told the War Cabinet: 'There must be more explanation, not only about the war situation but also about production, labour, wartime restrictions and the big problems that affect the life of everyone today'.[161] Only if the demands and motives of the various Departments of State were put clearly to the public would they put their maximum effort into the war. A 'Home Front Notebook' was produced with reference notes for speakers explaining the policies and necessary restrictions.[162] Leaflets entitled 'All on the Job' and 'A People at War' described the industrial war effort.[163] A pamphlet in question and answer form explained the clothes-rationing system (*fig. 21*).[164] An exhibition of utility furniture travelled round the country.[165]

All the publications emphasised the community of effort and the theme of individual sacrifice. For while the weekly reports often included grouses against queues and shortages, particularly of eggs, fruit and clothing, a significant report of March 1942 commented that 'people are willing to bear any sacrifice if a 100 per cent effort can be

Fig 21   Leaflet explaining the system of clothes rationing, 1942. INF 13/145/35. (*Continued overleaf*)

[158]INF 1/292 [159]INF 1/292 [160]INF 1/284 [161]INF CAB 66/23. WP (42) 155
[162]INF 2/4. 2962 [163]INF 2/2 [164]INF 13/145 [165]INF 1/297

Foreword
from the President of the Board of Trade

The people of this country can congratulate themselves on the results of clothe's rationing. In the first twelve months more than a quarter of a million tons of shipping space were saved in textiles alone. Nearly four hundred thousand men and women have been released from making cloth and clothing for civilians, and have gone into the Services or on to war production, while the workers that are left can be confident that they are making only the necessaries of war-time life.

The increasing strain of war on our supplies has made inevitable a cut in the clothing ration. But the cut is least for those whose needs are greatest, the children and the industrial workers.

Any sacrifice of comfort or appearance, which clothes rationing may bring to any of us, will, I am sure, be cheerfully borne, in order that victory may come sooner. Many patriotic people have returned unused coupons to the Board of Tráde thus helping our war effort by saving precious shipping space, material and labour. I hope that many more will do the same.

Hugh Dalton.

HOW
to use your clothing coupons

1. Your Coupons. Your Clothing Book contains 60 coupons, numbered 1–60 ; 20 of these are green, 20 brown and 20 red. (Each of them counts one only, despite the numbers printed on them). These 60 coupons are your ration for the current period from 1st June 1942.

In addition, you may have, or receive later, a supplementary sheet of 10 brown coupons (for children and workers in certain occupations) or one or two sheets of 10 green coupons (for certain older children, see para. 23).

Your name, address, and National Registration (Identity Card) Number must be written in ink on your Clothing Book. If you have not seen to this, you should do so at once.

These particulars must also be entered on any supplementary coupon sheets issued to you. If you are wise, you will pin these sheets inside the front cover of your Clothing Book—they cannot be replaced if you lose them.

2. When can I use my coupons? You can use your green coupons now, if you wish. You may not use the brown coupons until the 12th October, 1942, or the red coupons until a date which will be announced later. But there is no need for you to spend the green coupons before the 12th October—all the coupons in your Clothing Book will be valid *at least* until the 31st July, 1943.

The foregoing applies to the coupons in the supplementary sheets as well as to those in the Clothing Book.

3. Shopping. You must present coupons to buy clothing, cloth, footwear, and knitting yarn. Use your coupons for whatever clothing you need—but only if you *really* need it. You can shop anywhere without registration—the retailer will simply cut out the proper number of clothing coupons from your book and give it back to you. *Do not cut the coupons out yourself.* (It is illegal to sell or buy coupons, for this would defeat the purpose of "fair shares").

When using the coupons on a supplementary clothing coupon sheet you must hand your Clothing Book as well as the supplementary sheet to the shopkeeper.

4. Mail Orders. If you order goods by post, however, you must cut out the correct number of coupons yourself, sign your name clearly on the back, and post them, with the order. It is illegal to put such orders and coupons through the shopkeeper's letterbox. *They must be properly posted in a Post Office letter box.* If the retailer cannot supply you, you can either let him keep the coupons and order something else, or you can have them sent back. If you get them back they can only be used for another order by post. They will not be accepted over the counter.

5. Coupons saved from the last rationing period. If you still have some coupons left on your Clothing Card or on a supplementary clothing card issued to you during the last rationing period, you can use them at any time up to the 10th October. But "margarine" coupons can no longer be used.

The subject index is on page xxviii.

(59766) A 2

6. What Clothing Coupons look like.

Illustrations of the coupons for clothing are shown here for your guidance. The example depicts single coupons, but your coupons must not be cut from your Clothing Card, Clothing Book or supplementary clothing coupon sheet except by the shopkeeper or when you order goods by post. All these coupons have tinted backgrounds.

(*a*) Shows one of the coupons (green, brown and red, numbered 1–60) in your Clothing Book.

(*b*) Shows one of the coupons (brown, numbered C1–C10 or green, numbered C11–C20) on the various supplementary coupon sheets issued to children and young people.

(*c*) Shows one of the coupons (brown, numbered M1–M10) on the supplementary clothing coupon sheets which will be issued to workers in certain occupations.

(All the above coupons count 1 each, despite the numbers printed on them.)

(*d*) Shows the un-numbered coupons in the special Clothing Books which are being issued to certain personnel in H.M. Services (green or blue coupons) and to expectant mothers (blue coupons).

(Blue coupons are valid from the 1st June, like the green coupons in the ordinary Clothing Book.)

(*e*) & (*f*) are Emergency Coupon Vouchers, worth 5 and 2 coupons respectively issued in certain special cases, e.g. to people who have lost essential clothing in air raids and to workers in certain occupations.

(*g*) & (*h*) are the coupons on the Clothing Cards issued during the last ration period. These are valid only until the 10th October, 1942.

The large "strip ticket" types of Emergency Clothing Vouchers (not illustrated) printed on tinted paper in denominations of 10, 5, and 2 coupons will not be valid after the 10th October, 1942.

Coupons bearing the words "Isle of Man Clothing Coupon," issued by the Isle of Man Government under the Clothing Rationing Order, 1941 (corresponding to the 26 "margarine" coupons used in the United Kingdom last year) are no longer valid. Persons resident in the Isle of Man—which has its own clothes rationing scheme—are now given ration documents of the same kind as those used in the United Kingdom; these can be used in the United Kingdom, and similarly United Kingdom coupons can be used in the Isle of Man.

7. Number of coupons needed for the principal articles of adults' and children's clothing

The following table sets out the number of coupons needed for various articles of clothing, other than the following :—Infants' clothing (para. 8) ; industrial overalls (para. 9) ; industrial footwear (para. 10) ; officers' special uniform garments (para. 11) ; nurses' special garments (para. 12). The figures in the last column apply only to young children's wear which is exempt from Purchase Tax because of its size and character (not merely because it is Utility) ; the number of coupons needed depends on the garment—*not* on the age of the child.

Group I covers the following types of goods :—Woollen (i.e. containing more than 15 per cent. by weight of wool), fur, imitation fur, leather, imitation leather, corduroy (except Utility fustian cloths nos. 309, 310, 3090–1, 3100–3107), velvet, velveteen, and all pile fabrics except towelling. All other goods are in Group II. Saddle-lined garments are rated as unlined. Fur includes imitation fur.

	Man	Woman	★Child
Overcoat, Raincoat, etc.			
¶ Mackintosh, raincoat, overcoat, cape (except cycling cape), cloak—			
(*a*) if unlined, single texture, and Group II	9	9	7
(*b*) if fully lined and Group I	18	18	11
(*c*) other than those in (*a*) and (*b*)	16	15	10
Detached lining for overcoat, raincoat or mackintosh	7	7	4
Jacket, Cardigan, Waistcoat or Pullover			
§ Jacket, blouse-type jacket, sleeved waistcoat, coat, blazer, cycling cape, woman's half-length cape, woman's bolero—			
(*a*) if lined and Group I	13	12	8
(*b*) if unlined, single texture, and Group II	6	6	4
(*c*) if unlined, blouse-type and knitted	8	8	5
(*d*) other than those in (*a*), (*b*) or (*c*)	10	10	6
† Bolero, short jacket, short cape—			
(*a*) if Group I and with sleeves of not less than elbow length		5	
(*b*) if Group II and with no sleeves or with sleeves of less than elbow length		2	
(*c*) other than those in (*a*) or (*b*)		3	
Sweater, jersey, jumper, pullover, cardigan, woman's bedjacket—if Group I and weighing at least 10 ozs. (7 ozs. for children)	8	8	5
Cotton football jersey	4		2
Waistcoat, pullover, jumper, cardigan, woman's bedjacket, jersey, sweater—other than those described above	5	5	3
Trousers, Shorts or Skirt			
**Trousers, slacks, over-trousers, **breeches, jodhpurs—			
(*a*) if lined and Group I	11		8
(*b*) if unlined and Group II	5	5	4
(*c*) other than those in (*a*) or (*b*)	8	8	6
Shorts—			
(*a*) if fully-lined and Group I	6	6	4
(*b*) if not fully-lined and Group II	3	3	2
(*c*) other than those in (*a*) or (*b*)	5	5	3
Skirt, divided skirt—of Group I		6	4
Skirt, divided skirt—of Group II		4	3
Kilt (with or without bodice)	16	14	8

★ Young children's wear of a size, style and character, which is exempt from Purchase Tax, even if not Utility.
¶ Women's coats and capes fall into one of these categories if over 28 in. long.
§ Women's coats, capes and jackets fall into one of these categories if over 16 in. but not over 28 in. long.
† Not over 16 in. long, and not fur.
** Until December 31st, 1942, men's and youths' corduroy trousers and breeches may be sold at the Group II Coupon rating, even though not made from Utility fustian cloth, provided the price does not exceed 30s. retail (22s. 6d. wholesale) including Purchase Tax.

Continued on next page

Continued from previous page

	Man	Woman	★Child
Dress, Gown, Frock or Gym Tunic			
Dress, gown, frock—Group I, with sleeves of any length		11	8
Dress, gown, frock—Group II, with sleeves of any length		7	5
Gym tunic, skirt on bodice, sleeveless frock—Group I		8	6
Gym tunic, skirt on bodice, sleeveless frock—Group II		6	4
Shirt, Blouse or Shawl			
Shirt†—lined and/or woollen	7	7	6
Shirt†—unlined and not woollen	5	5	4
Blouse, shirt-blouse, shawl, plaid—Group I		6	4
Blouse, shirt-blouse, shawl, plaid—Group II		4	3
Blousette		2	2
Miscellaneous Garments			
One-piece shelter suit or like garment	11	11	8
Buster-suit or like garment			5
Cassock—woollen	8	8	7
Cassock—not-woollen	7	7	6
Overall ‡ or Apron ‡			
Apron (with or without bib) not over 3 sq. ft. in area	1	1	1
Apron (with or without bib) over 3 sq. ft. in area	2	2	2
Domestic smock overall, **sleeveless overall without tie fastening and with closed back (including non-industrial bib and brace overall)—Group II	6	6	4
Sleeveless overall with tie fastening and with closed back—Group II		4	4
Sleeveless overall with open back—Group II		3	3
** Overall with sleeves, other than domestic smock overall—Group II	7	7	5
Overall, Group I ; non-industrial boiler-suit	11	11	8
Dressing-Gown, House-Coat, Pyjamas, Nightdress, etc.			
Dressing-gown, house-coat—Group I	8	8	7
Dressing-gown, house-coat—Group II	7	7	6
Pyjama suit, nightshirt	8	8	6
Nightdress		6	5
Undergarments, etc.			
Combinations, petticoat, slip or like garment—woollen	7	6	4
Combinations, petticoat, slip or like garment—not woollen ; corselette	5	4	3
Suspender belt (not more than 10 in. in width at widest part), brassiere, bust bodice, modesty vest		1	1
Corsets	3	3	2
Vest, pants, or trunks with legs of any length—woollen ; vest with sleeves of any length, pants (long legs)—not woollen	4	3	2
Knickers or pantees (side length not over 18½ in.), men's legless trunks—not woollen ; sleeveless camisole ; body belt	2	2	2
Undergarment not elsewhere listed ; athlete's vest	3	3	2
Stockings, Socks, Collar, Tie, Handkerchief, etc.			
Pair of men's half-hose—not woollen ; pair of ankle-socks not exceeding 8 in. from point of heel to top of sock when not turned down	1	1	1
Pair of stockings or three-quarter hose or socks other than above—			
(*a*) Woollen	3	3	1
(*b*) Not woollen	3	2	1

★ Young children's wear of a size, style and character, which is exempt from Purchase Tax even if not Utility.
‡ For special rating of nurses' and industrial garments see paras. 9, 12, 29 and 34.
† With or without collar attached. § Knitted or woven body-belt without fastening or inner lining and not containing elastic or boning.
** Until December 31st, 1942, these types of overalls may be sold for 4 coupons, if the price does not exceed 9s. retail or 6s. 6d. wholesale (including Purchase Tax).

Continued on next page

Continued from previous page

	Man	Woman	★Child
Stockings, Socks, Collar, Tie, Handkerchief, etc.—*continued*			
Collar, shirt-front†, pair of cuffs, tie—of masculine type ; pair of sleeves¶	1	1	1
Sailor's collar	2		
Small handkerchief (of area less than 1 sq. ft.)	¼	¼	¼
Large handkerchief not more than 2 ft. in length or breadth	½	½	½
Bathing-Costume, Bathing Gown, etc.			
Bathing-gown—if Group I	8	8	7
Bathing-gown—if Group II	7	7	6
Bathing-costume	3	3	2
Bathing trunks—woollen	3		1
Cotton swimming drawers	1		1
Footwear,¶ Leggings, etc.			
Pair of goloshes, rubber overshoes, woman's rubber bootees, plimsolls, rope-soled shoes, low heeled slippers**, man's or boy's patent leather evening shoes, football boots, hockey boots or shoes, lacrosse boots or shoes, running shoes, race walking shoes or boots, boxing boots, cycling shoes or bowls shoes	4	4	2
Pair of sandals, non-industrial clogs or rubber-soled canvas shoes other than those listed above	5	5	2
Pair of boots, bootees, shoes, overshoes, overboots, high-heeled slippers, or footwear not described above (including cricket and golf)	7	5	3
Pair of leggings, gaiters or spats	3	3	2
Gloves, Scarf or Fur Garments			
Scarf or sash—over 5½ sq. ft. ; pair of gloves or mittens—containing leather or fur ; muff (other than fur)	2	2	2
Scarf or sash—not over 5½ sq. ft. ; pair of gloves or mittens—not containing leather or fur	1	1	1
Fur cape§, fur bolero§, short fur jacket§, fur stole or tie (other than fox), fur collar, fur muff (not over 12 in. length or breadth), pair of fur cuffs		5	
Fox fur stole or tie, mounted or unmounted ... *per skin*		5	

★ Young children's wear of a size, style and character, which is exempt from Purchase Tax even if not Utility.
** For women and girls, only those with heels not over 1½ in. high (measured from middle of side of heel, and including the thickness of the sole).
† With or without collar attached. § Not over 16 in. long.
¶ For special coupon rating of industrial and rubber footwear see para. 10 and para. 27.

8. Number of coupons needed for articles of infants' clothing

Items not on this list, such as scarves, handkerchiefs, gloves and shirts, have the same rating as for children. For meaning of 'Group I' and 'Group II' see note at top of previous table.

Description of Garment	Coupons needed	Maximum measurements
Overcoat, raincoat, mackintosh, cape—		*Overcoat* : 22" length from centre back collar seam to hem.
(*a*) fully-lined and Group I	7	
(*b*) unlined or saddle-lined and Group II	4	*Other items* : 26" length from centre back collar seam to hem.
(*c*) other than those in (*a*) or (*b*)	5	
Infant's shawl over 4 ozs.	4	
Matinee coat of woven material or short cape—not being *both* lined *and* Group I ; infant's shawl not over 4 ozs.	2	*Matinee coat or short cape* : 18" length from centre back collar seam to hem.
Jacket, blazer or like garment	4	26" chest.†
Cardigan, jersey, jumper, blouse, knitted matinee coat	2	*Cardigan or matinee coat* : 16" length § and 24" chest.† *Blouse* : 14" length.§ *Other items* : 18" length § and 24" chest.†

§ From centre shoulder to hem. † In the case of chest measurements the garment should be buttoned (if it has buttons) and measured across chest (1 in. below armpit), this figure being multiplied by two.

Continued on next page

(59766) A 3

Continued from previous page

Description of Garment	Coupons needed	Maximum measurements ("t" indicates length)
Knickers for outer wear (other than below), leggings with feet ... Legginettes, pantettes, gaiter overalls, breechettes, fully-lined knickers—		Knickers: 23" from top of waist (centre front) to crutch and thence to top of waist (centre back).
(a) Group I ...	3	Other garments: 26" overall length along outer side seam.
(b) Group II ...	2	
Unlined knickers for outer wear of woven Group I material ...	2	
Pair of gaiters ...	1	18" overall l. along outer side seam.
Skirt on bodice, skirt on straps ...	2	22" l. (centre shoulder to skirt hem).
Kilt on bodice ...	4	22" l. (centre shoulder to skirt hem).
Frock, pinafore frock, overall (except gaiter overalls), one-piece buster-suit, one-piece romper-suit or like garment (including sun-suit with bib); baby's day-gown—		Frock, pinafore frock or frock overall 22" length from centre shoulder to hem. Trouser overalls: 36" length t. Buster-suit, romper-suit or like garment: 22" length from centre shoulder to full length of garment when buttoned.
(a) Group II ...	2	
(b) knitted and weighing not more than 4 ozs. ...	2	
(c) other than in (a) and (b) ...	4	
Dressing-gown, baby-bag with sleeves, one-piece shelter suit or like garment ...	5	Dressing gown: 33" length from centre back collar seam to hem. Shelter suit or like garment: 38" length t.
Pyjama suit, sleeping-suit, night-dress, baby's nightgown—		Pyjama suit: 26" outside length of pyjama leg (waist to bottom of leg). Sleeping suit: 36" length from centre back collar seam to hem. Nightdress: 33" length t.
(a) Woollen ...	4	
(b) Not woollen ...	3	
Combinations, short petticoat, long petticoat, long flannel ...	2	Combinations or short petticoat: 22" length from centre shoulder to full length of garment.
Bodice, vest, trunks, knickers for underwear (including patch knickers), napkin, pilch ... (Waterproof knickers and pilches, and napkins of muslin are exempt)	1	Bodice: 15" length t. Vest: 22" length t. and 22" chest t. Trunks or knickers: 23" from top of waist (centre front) to crutch and thence to top of waist (centre back).
Pair of socks or knitted bootees or knitted shoes without leather sole ...	½	7" foot length from heel to point of toe.
Pair of stockings or three-quarter hose ...	2	7" foot length from heel to point of toe.
Pair of boots, shoes, overshoes, sandals or slippers—		
(a) under size 4 ...	1	
(b) Sizes 4 to 9 ...	2	
Bib or feeder without sleeves; pair of infantees without finger or thumb divisions; wrapper vest, body belt, knitted binder ...	½	(Note.—Infantees with finger or thumb division rank as gloves.)
Bib or feeder with sleeves; apron ...	1	Apron: 3 sq. ft. in area, excluding straps.

viii

---

9. Industrial Overalls

The special coupon ratings given below apply in general only to overalls of these types made from Utility Cloth Nos. 311, and 3110–3117 and marked accordingly. Until 31st December, 1942, however, other overalls of these types (except aprons) may be sold to retail customers (but not to traders) at the special coupon rates provided that they are unlined, are made of a plain or twill weave cotton material in a plain single colour in adults' sizes chargeable for purchase tax, and are sold at or below the price specified for such overalls in the general licence S.R. & O. 1942, No. 781. (See para. 29.)

	Coupons		Coupons
Boiler suit ...	4	Wrap-over coat overall ...	3
Bib and brace overall ...	3	Overall jacket or trousers ...	2
Overall long coat ...	3	Apron ...	2

10. Industrial and Rubber Footwear

The types of Footwear listed below, except clogs, are obtainable only by persons holding a buying permit. (See para. 27.)

	Coupons
Pair of rubber boots, knee length, three-quarter length or thigh length, excluding women's and children's varnished Wellingtons ...	4
Pair of rubber boots, of ankle-length, with integral tongue ...	2
Pair of rubber boots with textile leg ...	2
*Pair of industrial clogs ...	1
†Pair of industrial safety boots or shoes ...	4

* Subject to definitions contained in the War Emergency B.S. Definitions (See footnote to para. 16.)
† This does not cover ordinary heavy working boots.

11. Special Uniform Garments of a type normally worn by Officers
of the British, Dominion and Allied Forces (including Women's Services) and of the Merchant Navy (British and Foreign)

	Coupons		Coupons
Trench-coat ...	30	Trousers, breeches, whether woollen	
Overcoat (incl. "British warm") ...	25	or not ...	8
Battle-dress ...	20	Kilt ...	16
Tunic or naval jacket—		Skirt, whether woollen or not ...	6
(a) woollen ...	16	Shorts whether woollen or not ...	5
(b) not woollen ...	9	Cap ...	2

12. Nurses' Special Garments

The coupon ratings given below apply to special garments of the type worn by nurses, whether the customer is a nurse or not; thus, a housemaid's apron of this type requires 4 coupons.

	Coupons
White apron with bib of a type worn by nurses ...	4
White cotton overall of a type worn in coat or wrap-over style with long or short sleeves ...	8
Unlined dress of a type worn by nurses of plain or twill weave cotton in navy or butcher blue or of nurse cloth ...	8
Lined dress of a type worn by nurses of plain or twill weave cotton in navy or butcher blue or of nurse cloth ...	11
Head square ...	2

ix

---

reached and the burden fairly borne by all'.[166] Rationing, explained in a very full pamphlet equally useful to the wartime public and future historians, was welcomed rather than resented by the public: it meant fair shares for rich and poor. Stafford Cripps, later Lord Privy Seal in the reconstituted Cabinet of February 1942 (and a vegetarian tee-totaller, devoutly religious with a stern sense of duty), had been right to persuade Churchill that it was an acceptable policy.[167] Few grumbles were reported as rationing was gradually extended to clothing and to more foods, the meat allowance reduced and a 'points' system intro-duced for tinned and then other foods such as rice and cereals (*table of events, endpapers*). A secret memorandum to the Minister from the Director of the Home Department in May 1942 reported that 'the heavier penalties for black marketeers, the promise of restrictions on luxury meals, the extension of points rationing, the abolition of basic petrol . . . have been welcomed as real evidence that the government is in earnest'.[168] Morale was recovering after the disasters of February.

The public were willing to accept shortages and restrictions so long as the principle of 'fair shares' was respected and so long as the government took the lead in economies and was efficient in organising them. Restrictions on the use of paper were welcomed until government departments were themselves seen to be wasting paper.[169] In fact the salvage campaign – after complaints of inefficient collection were remedied – produced vast quantities of scrap. The earlier wordy posters (*fig. 9*) were replaced by Fougasse's simple series of cartoons announcing that paper, metal or rubber 'helps to make munitions'.[170] Leaflets and 'notes for speakers' were produced in response to the

---

[166]INF 1/292   [167]INF 2/5   [168]INF 1/284   [169]INF 1/292   [170]INF 3/197-200

Home Division's warning in May 1942 that 'If fuel rationing proposals are to meet with greater acceptance further explanations of the need for them must be given'.[171] There was a good response to the broadcasting and poster campaign on behalf of the Ministry of Fuel and Power: pictures of factory workers and families wasting gas and electricity seemed to inspire the desired guilt[172] (*fig. 23*). Even the caption 'Don't be Fuel-ish' was well received. In the discussions on the White Paper on coal in May 1942 the Cabinet decided public response was good enough to make compulsory rationing unnecessary.[173]

The only revolt came with the miners' strikes in the spring of 1944. Fuel-saving propaganda was described as 'a lost cause'. The public felt strongly that instead of threatening them with dire measures if they increased fuel consumption the government should have been threatening the miners.[174] In any case housewives were angry at being asked to economise when their allocation was already too meagre to keep them warm. They were angry, too, at the tactlessness of some of the Ministry of Food's recipes recommending ingredients they could not afford.[175] But ideas for Woolton pies, films and broadcasts aimed at women 'on the kitchen front' were informative, useful and generally well received. So were the instructions to 'Make do and Mend' by 'Mrs Sew-and-Sew' and to 'Dig for Victory' in every available inch of the garden and allotment[176] (*fig. 22*). The press carried gardening hints and pictures of vegetables growing in the moat of the Tower of London.[177] The farming press was full of information, placed on behalf of the Ministry of Agriculture, on the best methods of stock breeding and tillage, telling farmers to manure well, plant early and look after their machines.[178] Posters encouraged everyone to join their village produce associations, make compost heaps and generally 'lend a hand on the land'.[179] Many accepted the suggestions in the press to spend their holidays in volunteer agricultural camps.[180] Home Intelligence reports of the summer of 1943 mentioned the interest shown in the 'holidays on the land' scheme.[181] The previous year the 'stay at home' campaign had coincided disastrously with the running of special holiday excursion trains. 'Anger and disgust' with the government had been reported; and Bracken told the War Cabinet that 'This subject has been fixed upon by the public as a typical example of government muddle'.[182] More successful at cutting the use of public transport were the posters asking 'Is your journey really necessary?' and the encouragement to walk to work – or 'Go by Shank's Pony'[183] (*fig. 24*). The cheeky pony with a shoe for a body became as familiar a figure as the malevolent swastika-marked creature inciting the public to spend: the squanderbug was reported to make a powerful impact but was considered offensive by a minority.[184] In fear of repeating the mistake of spreading trepidation as in the anti-rumour propaganda, the Ministry preferred to concentrate on a straightforward War Savings campaign.

Fig 22   Poster in the food production campaign, using one of the most famous slogans of the war. INF 13/140/22.

Fig 23   Poster by H.M. Bateman in the fuel saving campaign, 1942. INF 13/146/3. (*See overleaf*).

Fig 24   Poster in the 'Shanks' Pony' campaign. INF 3/90. (*See overleaf*).

[171]INF 1/284 [172]INF 13/146 [173]INF 1/921 [174]INF 1/292 [175]INF 1/293
[176]INF 2/72 [177]INF 2/1 [178]INF 2/60 [179]INF 2/60 [180]INF 2/60 [181]INF 1/292
[182]CAB 66/28. WP (42) 385 [183]INF 2/72 [184]INF 1/292

Your own vegetables all the year round...

if you

DIG FOR VICTORY NOW

THE DAUGHTER WHO HEAPED ON THE *COAL*

SAVE FUEL
FOR BATTLE

ISSUED BY THE MINISTRY OF FUEL AND POWER

PRINTED FOR H.M STATIONERY OFFICE BY CHROMOWORKS LTD. LONDON 51- 4209.

USE SHANKS' PONY

WALK
when you can

AND EASE THE BURDEN WHICH WAR PUTS ON TRANSPORT

The Ministry was perhaps most successful in its role of instructor when it acted as publicity agent for the Ministry of Health. Pamphlets explaining the necessity of immunisation against diphtheria were distributed to the public by Local Authorities and followed up in June 1942 by an intensive press campaign costing £20000.[185] The stricken baby in the posters over the caption 'Protect your Child' was as effective in bringing clients into the clinics as the skeleton-like figure of another poster warning against venereal disease.[186] Tactfully titled films like 'Health is a Victory' and 'In Defence of the Nation' carried the same message. Officials seemed surprised at the public approval of the VD campaign and at the response to the appeal for blood donors – even at the request to trap their germs in their handkerchieves (*fig. 1*). They were less impressed by the reaction to their campaign on behalf of the Ministry of Labour to increase production. Bracken told the War Cabinet categorically that 'General appeals to the public or particular sections of it to work harder should not be made'. Most were working to the limit of their capacity and would dislike any implication to the contrary: 'We must stop appealing to the public or lecturing it. One makes it furious, the other resentful'.[187] He preferred the industrial campaign to rest on explanation by leaflets explaining the necessity for more munitions and the economics of production and consumption.[188] But during a time of low morale like the first half of 1943 when the excitement of El Alamein and Stalingrad had worn off and there seemed no sign of the invasion of Italy, such informative low-key propaganda made little impression. The film 'Desert Victory' was more successful in keeping enthusiasm alive than 'Strategy of Manpower' – in spite of a budget of £2000 – in encouraging volunteers into war work.

Home Intelligence weekly reports that spring complained of 'apathy and indifference' among workers. The main effect of the Essential Work Orders had been to deprive managers of the weapon of the threat of dismissal; slacking increased. There was said to be 'a complete absence of understanding among many work people that this is their war'.[189] The Ministry resorted once more to exhortation. Posters in the dockyards begged dockers to 'Speed up Loading and Unloading' and achieve a 'Quicker Turnround'.[190] And in the factories they announced 'It's your personal war' under contrasting pictures of German workers at their machines and the British drinking tea[191] (*fig. 26*). Production like morale, went up not with the poster but with the boost of the invasion and then the surrender of Italy.

[185]INF 1/344 [186]INF 2/71 [187]CAB 66/23. WP (42) 155 [188]INF 2/7
[189]INF 1/292 [190]INF 2/71 [191]INF 2/72

Fig 25 Poster in one of the campaigns to recruit women for war service. INF 3/403.

TIME IS PRECIOUS

for each Mr COLEMAN ······ there is DIPL·ING· KAUFMANN

for each PHYLLIS BROWN ····· there is PAULA BRAUN

for each BILL SMITH   there is WILHELM SCHMIDT

YOUR OPPOSITE NUMBER WORKS FAST
YOU MUST BEAT HIM

IT'S YOUR PERSONAL

WAR

7. Reconstruction 1940-5: Idealism or Bribery?

CRIMINAL

As older men were conscripted into the forces, more women had to be persuaded to 'Come into the Factories'[192] (*fig. 25*). 'Victory is in *your* hands' shouted a poster of women carrying out intricate tasks in a munitions factory.[193] The 1944 pamphlet 'Fifty Facts about Women' showed them at work as drivers, postmen and engineers as well as on the land, in industry and the forces.[194] This was a strikingly different picture from the one that emerges from the Ministry documents at the beginning of the war. Then, women had been considered vulnerable, needing cups of tea during air raids, special broadcasts on 'The Kitchen Front', articles on 'Looking Our Best' and 'Being Brave', and films on 'Neighbours under Fire'. The longer documentary 'They Also Serve' was planned to show 'a day in the life of a housewife spent entirely in the ungrumbling service of her family who are doing war work'. Women living alone were feared to be the weak link in the chain of morale. 'Miss Grant Goes to the Door', a five-minute short, showed a single woman behaving courageously during a raid. Public attitudes, as well as those of the officials, changed towards working women as the war progressed. In November 1940 there was resentment towards women without domestic responsibilities who were avoiding war work. By March 1944 Home Intelligence investigators found that men were suspicious of women workers, fearing they would deprive them of their jobs after the war.[195] The text of pamphlets like 'Eve in Overalls' certainly stressed the future participation of women in industry.[196]

Bracken had told the War Cabinet in the bleak autumn of 1942 that 'post-war conditions seem to be more a cause of anxiety as to what they may bring to the individual in the shape of unemployment and distress than of hope for the blessings that they may bring to the nation at large'.[197] Officials tended to exaggerate the public's fear of the future. Their advocacy of social reform was thus part of their early policy of reassurance as much as of any great reforming zeal. It was also an attempt to buy off antagonism to the government. For in June 1940 the Home Morale Emergency Committee reported to the Policy Committee that 'class feeling' was a major threat to public calm.[198] Officials had shown how class conscious they were in their early patronising picture of the average Englishman as a sturdy peasant. They had considered directing a different 'anger campaign' to each 'class'. They were worried by a Home Intelligence report that 'a striking trend seems to be

[192]INF 13/126 [193]INF 13/126 [194]INF 2/5 [195]INF 1/292 [196]INF 2/2
[197]CAB 66/29. WP (42) 459 [198]INF 1/250

Fig 26   An example of a poster in one of the more exhortatory campaigns mounted by the Ministry of Information. INF 2/72.

increased ill feeling towards the upper classes who are accused of being the first to leave bombed districts, of taking the best places in reception areas and of refusing to accommodate poorer refugees'.[199] In June 1941 another report called the attention of the Home Planning Committee 'to the widespread irritation caused in country districts that evacuees were not billeted in the larger homes'.[200] Complaints by East Enders after a particularly bad raid that 'it is always the poor that get it' made the men in the Ministry almost grateful for a direct hit on Buckingham Palace. Forty journalists were immediately despatched to inspect and report the damage. They managed to arouse sympathy for the Royal Family. As shortages increased, the Home Planning Committee thought it advisable to run a campaign pointing out that they were not due to discrimination in favour of the middle class emphasising the need for equal sacrifices by all.[201]

Resentment of the rich by the poor was a continual theme of the Home Intelligence weekly reports until the end of the war, particularly in the form of grumbles about the black market.[202] A film on the topic was abandoned because of its anti-semitic overtones and because it might have given away too many ideas for evading restrictions.[203] Just as rationing was welcomed as bringing fair shares, so there was an outcry at the suggestion late in 1944 that the points system might be abolished: only the rich could benefit. But the grouses were a natural reaction to restrictions and did not in fact constitute any great threat to the government or to the war effort. Complaints at high maximum prices allowed in restaurants or at the rich evading their responsibilities towards the refugees hardly justified the fear apparent in the Ministry's Policy Committee discussions of some kind of people's uprising.[204] All left-wing views were suspect, journals and public meetings scrutinised for subversive ideas. Waterfield even considered it slightly risky to take on Francis Williams as Director of Press and Public relations in May 1941 because 'he is, of course, a socialist'.[205] Fear of communism influenced the Ministry's pro-Russian propaganda. And the poster designs of the woman calling her sisters into the factories betrayed the belief that the public were in sympathy with the socialist cause (*fig. 25*).

The elitist heads of the Ministry may have overestimated the danger of a populist rising. Fear certainly encouraged the Policy Committee in June 1940 to discuss the possibility of 'redressing grievances and inequalities and to create new opportunities'. Kenneth Lee raised the specific question of post-war social reform.[206] Under pressure from Duff Cooper, the War Cabinet in August set up a War Aims Committee (WAC). Its terms of reference instructed it 'to make suggestions in regard to a post-war European and world system' and 'to consider means of perpetuating the national unity achieved in this country during the war through a social and economic structure designed to secure equality of opportunity and service among all classes of the

[199]INF 1/292   [200]INF 1/249   [201]INF 1/251   [202]INF 1/292   [203]INF 1/250
[204]INF 1/913   [205]INF 1/37   [206]INF 1/848

community'.[207] The long memorandum produced by Duff Cooper for
the WAC with the help of Arnold Toynbee was gradually watered
down so that practical suggestions for rebuilding, social services and
family allowances became vague platitudes.[208] Churchill's lack of
interest and the end of the blitz had an equal effect on reforming zeal.
When Arthur Greenwood, the chairman of the WAC vetoed the
subjects put forward by MOI officials for BBC talks because 'Peace
aims' and 'A new World Order' were too provocative, Nicolson and
Radcliffe put up little opposition. They agreed that 'people want to win
the war, not the peace'.[209] Nor did the Ministry encourage *Picture Post*
to produce a sequel to its successful issue on 'A Plan for Britain' of
January 1941.

A year later a Ministry paper declared the Minister to be 'concerned
to promote discussion and publication of the government's reconstruction programme'. But it added the rider that 'it is his duty to
prevent the ventilation of topics which might impair morale'.[211] The
succession of William Jowitt and then John Anderson to Greenwood as
Chairman of the Reconstruction Committee – and then in November
1943 the creation of a special Ministry of Reconstruction under Lord
Woolton – indicated the growing prestige of the topic. But within the
MOI the emphasis on post-war social reforms decreased as confidence
in the public grew. Officials realised their fears of a people's uprising
were unfounded. A Home Intelligence survey in the depressing month
of June 1942 – just before the censure motion on Churchill following
the Battle of Tobruk – reported that the majority of the public wished
to concentrate on winning the war and only later think about peace
aims.[212] Too much talk about reconstruction would only encourage a
movement for reform. Bracken voiced his doubts about publicity for the
Beveridge plan for comprehensive social insurance to a sympathetic
Prime Minister.[213] And after the report had been rapturously received
by the public – according to the Home Intelligence report, 'the most
discussed topic in recent times' – the Ministry refused requests from
Local Information committees for speakers on the subject.[214] In January
1945 Regional Information Officers were still told that 'the Director
General had expressed the view that MOI meetings were not the right
method of satisfying the public demand for information about HMG
plans for the future'.[215] Forbidden topics included international as well
as national post-war reconstruction. Frustrated, public enthusiasm
turned to cynicism. The survey commissioned by R.A. Butler on his
plan for widening educational opportunities received a mild response
after post-Beveridge hopes had been dashed.[216] Nevertheless, the early
enthusiasm of the Ministry for a constructive social policy – whatever
its motive – had been responsible for the work of the successive
reconstruction committees. Woolton's Ministry gave Labour leaders
Attlee, Bevin and Morrison a platform from which they could air their
reconstruction ideas. The public listened. Home Intelligence reports

---

[207]CAB 66/11. WP (40) 332 [208]PREM 4/87/10 [209]INF 1/177 [210]INF 1/234
[211]INF 1/864 [212]INF 1/293 [213]PREM 4/89/2 [214]INF 1/73 [215]INF 1/301 [216]INF 1/293

noted in March 1944 that government plans for the future were being criticised as 'too woolly'.[217] In the election the following May the public made their choice.

While propaganda for social reform declined, Bracken and his officials were getting on with their task of explanation and information. The growing optimism of the early months of 1944 received a set-back with the arrival of the terrifying flying bombs. Home Intelligence reports noted that Londoners were 'weary, strained and anxious'. They demanded factual information and were given leaflets telling them how to help the victims of the new weapons.[218] Complaints that housing repairs were too slow and inefficient were met by advertisements in the press on behalf of the Ministry of Labour asking women to come and cook for the builders.[219] The government, through the Ministry, was expected to give instructions and take responsibility for all aspects of life. The public's expectation that it should do so, its acceptance of increased bureaucracy, had grown at the same rate as the Ministry's new faith in the public. In March 1944 an Official Committee on the Machinery of Government felt it 'necessary to impress the value of MOI pretty strongly on Ministers'. After 'an unfortunate start . . . they have now built up an organisation and developed a technique which are impressive in the extreme'.[220] Officials had learnt the lesson that no amount of propaganda could raise morale if bombs were falling and people hungry and homeless, or change basic attitudes to communism or capitalism. On the other hand they had discovered that taking people into their confidence and giving them information made a surprising difference to public co-operation. For most impressive of all was the new insistence on the ability of the people to fight their own war if only given the necessary explanations. A study of the Ministry's archive brings out most clearly this change of attitude of the officials towards the public – from patronage and fear to partnership and respect.

[217]INF 1/292 [218]INF 13/219 [219]INF 2/65 [220]INF 1/941

Suggestions for further reading

HAVE-NOTS

Background
Paul Addison. *The Road to 1945*. Cape 1975.
Angus Calder. *The People's War*. Cape 1971.
Anthony Rhodes. *Propaganda – The Art of Persuasion 1933-45*. Chelsea House 1979.
A.J.P. Taylor. *English History 1914-45*. Oxford University Press 1965.
Philip M. Taylor. *The Projection of Britain: British overseas publicity and propaganda 1919-1939*. Cambridge University Press 1981.
R.H. Titmuss. *Problems of Social Policy*. HMSO 1950.
Francis Williams. *Parliament, Press and People*. Heinemann 1946.

The Ministry
Sir Fife Clark. *The Central Office of Information*. Allen & Unwin 1970.
Ian Mclaine. *Ministry of Morale*. Allen & Unwin 1979.

The Media
C.K. Bird. *A School of Porpoises*. Methuen 1946.
Asa Briggs. *The History of Broadcasting in the UK:* Vol III; *The War of Words*. Oxford University Press 1970.
Forsyth Hardy. *Grierson on Documentary*. Faber 1979.
Roger Manvell. *Film*. Penguin 1946.

Memoirs and Diaries
Duff Cooper. *Old Men Forget*. Rupert Hart Davis 1953.
Hugh Dalton. *The Fateful Years 1931-45*. Frederick Muller 1957.
David Dilks (ed.). *The Cadogan Diaries*. Cassell 1971.
John Harvey (ed.). *The Diplomatic Diaries of Oliver Harvey 1937-40*. Collins 1970.
David Low. *Autobiography*. Michael Joseph 1956.
Lord Macmillan. *A Man of Law's Tale*. Macmillan 1953.
Nigel Nicolson (ed.). *Diaries and letters of Harold Nicolson*. Weidenfeld & Nicolson 1970.
J.C.W. Reith. *Into the Wind*. Hodder & Stoughton 1949.
Charles Stuart (ed.). *The Reith Diaries*. Collins 1975.

Biographies
Lord Birkenhead. *Walter Monckton*. Weidenfeld & Nicolson 1969.
Andrew Boyle. *Poor Dear Brendan – the Quest for Brendan Bracken*. Hutchinson 1974.

Alan Bullock. *The Life and Times of Ernest Bevin Vol II: Minister of Labour*. Heinemann 1967.

José Harris. *Beveridge*. Oxford University Press 1977.

A.J.P. Taylor. *Beaverbrook*. Hamish Hamilton 1972.

J.W. Wheeler-Bennett. *John Anderson, Viscount Waverley*. Macmillan 1962.

Printed in the UK for HMSO. Dd. 717089 C50 2/83.

	1939	**1940**	**1941**
January		8 Rationing introduced in Britain (beginning with butter, bacon and sugar)	21 DAILY WORKER closed dow
February			
March			5 Essential Work Orders introduced
April			
May		10 Chamberlain resigns Churchill Prime Minister 'Home Guard' formed 22 Emergency powers introduced 29 Dunkirk Evacuation	10 Rudolf Hess flies from Germany to Scotland
June		10 Italy declares war on Britain and France 17 Fall of France	– Introduction of clothes rationing 22 Germany invades Russia
July			
August		8 Battle of Britain begins 23 Beginning of the Blitz	
September	1 Germany invades Poland 2 British National Service Bill in force, enabling men aged 18 to 41 to be called up 3 Britain and France declare war on Germany		22 'Tanks for Russia' week begins in British arms factories
October			
November		14 Bombing raid on Coventry	
December			7 Japanese attack Pearl Harbour 8 Britain and USA declare w on Japan 10 PRINCE OF WALES and REPULSE sunk by Japanese 11 USA enters war against Germany and Italy